INCLUSIVISM™

The World on the Brink
of a Social Revolution

S.A. Nitz

Order this book online at www.trafford.com
or email orders@trafford.com

Most Trafford titles are also available at major online book retailers.

Printed in the United States of America.

ISBN: 978-1-4251-5713-5 (sc)
ISBN: 978-1-4269-6779-5 (hc)

Library of Congress Control Number: 2011907039

Trafford rev. 08/03/2011

 www.trafford.com

North America & international
toll-free: 1 888 232 4444 (USA & Canada)
phone: 250 383 6864 ♦ fax: 812 355 4082

For
all of the friends
and family members
I have lost along the way

TABLE OF CONTENTS

Table of Illustrations

Acknowledgements

Thanks to:

Professor Dr. Heiner Monheim, of the University of Trier for help and support in the research process.

Marco Foz, former President of Radio Aktiv, for providing me with a platform to discuss my ideas with international decision makers.

My family, for their support of this work and my person as well as the passing on of relevant information and tips which I might otherwise have missed.

The love of my life.

Chapter One
BIRTH PAINS

The Beginning of the Metamorphosis

"Punishment is now unfashionable...because it creates moral distinctions among men, which, to the democratic mind, are odious. We prefer a meaningless collective guilt to a meaningful individual responsibility." Thomas Szasz

There is no question that the world is currently in the middle of a prolonged period of social, political and environmental disruption. The developed world is facing an economic crisis, the scale of which has never been seen before. The developing world is facing massive political and social unrest. The wealthy seem to be getting wealthier and the poor, poorer.

High level executives earn salaries that are thousands of times that which their employees earn, a development of the last 20 years. Bankers receive exorbitant bonuses for taking uncalculated risks, but are not held accountable when these risks result in massive failures. Companies neglect infrastructure maintenance and safety requirements in an effort to boost short term profits and, when the inevitable disaster happens, display incompetance and distain for the public and the environment at large by pointing fingers and trying to shift the blame.

Politicians seek to maintain the support of their donor base by consistently promoting the interests of lobbyists and big business over those of the citizens. When faced with massive opposition by the voting

9

public, the people are stamped as ignorant and unable to grasp the scope of the problems at hand. The political establishment blatantly ignores the wishes of its citizens. As a result, voter apathy increases and voter participation at elections plummets.

The voting process on the whole is treated with distain; election results are rigged; the opposition is ridiculed and in some cases violently oppressed. Should a reform candidate succeed in being elected, despite voting manipulation, the formerly elected official may just ignore the decision of the public and refuse to hand over power. Other political innovators are simply incarcerated or even killed: their right to expression squelched by the political machinery.

People in positions of authority misuse their power to promote personal agendas; either financial, political or in the worst cases, sexual. When confronted with these abuses of power, the perpetrators deny responsibility and, in many cases, seem to consider their behavior as being part of the rewards of their position. The offender tries to avoid being held accountable and instead, the public at large is called to bear the consequences of the moral failures.

The effect of this general state of affairs is demoralization across the entire expanse of society. Public unrest, mass protests, strikes and violent demonstrations are the openly visible signs of this condition. In certain extreme cases, irate individuals direct their frustration and anger at the general state of affairs towards individual power holders and assassinations, and assassination attempts occur as a result. But there are other less visible signs. A massive increase in the level of criminal activity, psychologically related health problems and suicides can also be documented.

On the lowest level, discontent and unhappiness with life in general often leads to a decline in the quality of goods and services, because the people providing them have lost all personal motivation and pride. Nevertheless, an enormous increase in the consumption of mass public entertainment and the monumental increase in the production and use of computer games and various game platforms provides the disenfranchised citizen with a means of escaping reality. These are simply another form of tranquilizer and can prove to be just as addictive as drugs and alcohol, the use of which has skyrocketed in certain segments of society.

In general, this is a very dismal state of affairs and the tendency might be to resign as a result. However, the situation is actually not as bad as it seems. In fact, these societal circumstances are just an indication of the emergence of a new social form. Moreover, as is the case when a child is born, this social form, Inclusivism™, is *also* being heralded by a series of intense and very painful contractions.

The coming social revolution is being presaged by the emergence of a new breed of societal member. The presence and increasing prominence within a culture of these people; dubbed Digital Nomads, Cultural Creatives, Global Citizens, the Creative Class and, by this author, the New Independent Problem Solvers is one of the main indicators of the metamorphosis of society from Capitalism to Inclusivism™. As the main protagonists of the values of the new social form, the steady increase in their numbers and their influence is shifting and changing everything in society.

Being members of society with a growing significance, they are also affecting the built environment. The emergence of alternative planning and building schemes such as Sensible Growth, Anti – Sprawl, and New Urbanism mark a decided shift in societal principles with respect to the usage of natural resources within communities. The growing economic and political clout of these people has also led to a modification of values within the business community and, as a result, the ideas of Natural Capitalism and Sustainability have gained mounting importance.

Many notable examples of the changes within the built environment can be found all over the world. Chief among these are the cities of Seaside and Celebration in Florida, USA and the city of Curitiba, Brazil. Curitiba, where Sustainability is a highly-prized value among the citizenry, was not only applied to the buildings and the city planning, but also to the entire social structure. These cities serve not only as examples of the application of ideals touted by these increasingly important societal members, they also serve as an illustration of the changes which will come upon society in general as this paradigm shift permeates all aspects of life on this planet.

Within the business sector, the emergence and increasing influence of the New Independent Problem Solvers has led to the formation of a movement to radically increase efficiency in the usage and application of resources both natural and human. This movement, dubbed the Factor Ten Club, reached a high point during a conference in the French village of Carnoules where the principles of the group were recorded in a publication called the "Carnoules Declaration". Since then, these standards have been quietly being accepted and implemented in business as well as governmental institutions throughout the world.

Although many different scientists have acknowledged the emergence of this new breed of citizen and their increasing importance within society, until now, none of them had been able to explain where they have come from. Some scientists have suggested that the New Independent Problem Solvers are synonymous for artists. Others have used the frequency of gays within a community as an indicator to determine their prevalence. However, by bringing together the collected works of two U.S. scientists of the previous century, the synergy created yields the solution to the conundrum.

Abraham Maslow, one of the most well-known human psychologists of the last century, postulated that human behavior could be explained by coming to the understanding that each action taken by a person is undertaken to fulfill intrinsic human needs. Once having fulfilled the lower needs, to the greatest extent, the person then seeks to fulfill higher needs. In all, Maslow determined that there were five levels of human needs. Graphically depicted, this theory became widely know as Maslow's Pyramid of Needs.

Parallel to Maslow, another scientist was trying to determine and categorize human personalities through experiments conducted on his students. After many years of observations and experiments, this scientist, Clare W. Graves, determined that human personalities could be classified into categories. Likewise, he also discovered that human beings move through a string of personality categories as they progress.

Upon thorough comparison of the two theories propounded by Maslow and Graves, similarities emerge. Both scientists suggested that human personalities develop in a series of successive steps and that the further along in the progression a person was, the more fully human or advanced that person became. Both also discovered that the state of the physical environment in which these people found themselves, coupled with their life experiences, would determine where they were within this evolutionary process. Finally, both scientists determined that there was a decided difference between people currently in the lower developmental stages and those breaking through a certain level of advancement.

Whereas Maslow developed his theories based primarily upon observation, Graves produced his ideas based upon experimental results. The most astounding finding of this research was that the problem-solving capacity of people grew exponentially at the higher levels of development. When compared to the other developmental levels, the higher levels produced many times more and much better solutions to problems posed.

Placing these findings back in the context of the search for the cause of the increase in number of New Independent Problem Solvers, the answer is quickly found. The shift in societal values documented by Ronald Inglehart and the emergence of

14

Digital Nomads, Cultural Creatives, Global Citizens, the Creative Class or the Independent Problem Solvers is an indication of the general level of advancement of society. These people are not an anomaly or fluke of nature. Fact is, that they are simply normal individuals who have undergone a radical transformation of their thinking processes. This change in thought processing can take place in two ways.

Firstly, a revolution in thinking processes can be brought about by the environment in which the individual finds himself. Placed in a wholesome and nurturing environment, an individual will begin a process of internal growth and development. Ultimately this process of self-reflection will bring about an awakening to wider issues outside the realm of personal, individual well-being and will result in the spiritual and psychological awakening of the individual.

Secondly, an individual can go through this change by beginning on a course of self-reflection and truth-seeking. In this case the process is usually initiated either through a traumatic personal experience, or a life-changing spritual one. Having received this impetus, the internal growth and transformational process is remarkably similar to that in the first scenario, however the final impact is different.

Once having undergone the alteration process, the person will then begin to have a profound effect on his immediate environment, seeking to improve quality of life conditions in his community and beyond. These improvements will then provide an environment which fosters the thought development processes in other members of the community. The sequences are reciprocal in nature. Either the environment will initiate the transformational process, or the person, once having gone through this revolution in thought, will ultimately change his environment. Which ever way this alteration comes about, change is inevitable and contagious.

By examining the effect that this growing number of individuals is having on existing society, the future of society in general can then be anticipated. Additionally, a careful investigation of the values of these societal members must be undertaken. This is necessary in order to generate a more thorough comprehension of the morals and ideals driving their actions. After studying the effects that this group is already having on their environment and obtaining a deep-seated understanding of their moral fibre, it will then be possible to speculate on the outcome of the social revolution which is about to take place.

These Independent Problem Solvers, when put into positions of authority, can then be expected to implement sweeping changes in their environments. Based upon their values, these alterations will almost certainly be conducive to the advancement of society, in general, as well as the cultivation of the progression of the individual, specifically.

Therefore, the emergence and development of the Independent Problem Solvers should not be greeted with scepticism. Instead, their appearance should be met with excitement, as they are the key to shedding the now obviously obsolete societal form of Capitalism and to the advancement of the new social form of Inclusivism™.

Chapter Two

SIGNS OF CHANGE

Social Indicators of the Conversion

"Innovation distinguishes between a leader and a follower."
Steve Jobs

2.1 Digital Nomads and the Creative Class

The Digital Nomad

In their now famous book, <u>Digital Nomad</u> from 1997, the authors Tsugio Makimoto & David Manners explored the future of civilization in light of the advances in communication technologies. Their thesis stated that through the improvements in both hardware and software technologies, mankind will be able to rekindle the nomadic lifestyle which it followed for hundreds of thousands of years before settling into a more sedentary lifestyle 10,000 years ago. "That is the nature of the revolution which is going to give people options on a scale never seen before. With the ability to tap into every worldwide public information source from anywhere on the globe, and the ability to talk to anyone via a video link, humans are going to be given the opportunity, if they want it, of being global nomads."[1]

This creates an interesting set of problems for societies in general. If the best paid and most qualified workers are no longer bound through geography to their workplace, then they can choose to

---

[1] Makimoto, Tsugio; Manners, David, Digital Nomad, pg. 6

live anywhere in the world or, in extreme cases, nowhere in the world for any length of time. A government can then be faced with the prospect of losing its tax base and its most desirable citizens. "Given political and economic freedom to travel freely, people would have freedom to choose to which establishment they will pay their taxes. Administrations might have to compete for citizens! Of course governments would all want the rich or high-earning ones, which could lead to some interesting countries. For instance, all the rich people would live in countries with low tax and few social services, and all the poor people would want to live in Scandinavia!!"[2]

The idea of living wherever one would like to is not new. Certain segments of society have been capable of just that for the longest time. The wealthier segment of society has always been a great proponent of travel and multiple living spaces. That is how they earned the name the "Jet Set".

Throughout history, certain developments caused an increase in the level of mobility which in turn facilitated a more transient lifestyle. The first such invention was the steam powered locomotive, thereafter the automobile. This newly created freedom caused the garden city movement in the late 1800's and following this, the great expanse of suburbia. Both of these community forms, in turn, loosened the traditional ties between a major city and its inhabitants.

During the span of the next decades, according to the authors of Digital Nomad, humanity, or at least

[2] Makimoto, Tsugio; Manners, David, Digital Nomad, pg 23

the people who are capable of dealing with the coming technology, will have incomes which enable it to live wherever in the world it chooses. The majority of the people on the planet will also have the ability and means to be able to travel wherever it wants. People will no longer be tied to a specific location due to an occupation. Instead, the most ardent proponents of this new lifestyle will have multiple homelands and homes during their lifetimes.

In the past we had to live where we worked. In the future, we will work where we live. "So, when we are all liberated from the geographical ties of home and office, what energies will be released and how will we use them? What will happen if we can work anywhere? Will we prefer Pittsburgh to Phuket? Osaka to Bermuda? Liverpool to Provence? Frankfurt to Bali?...It's anyone's guess, but there's a fair chance that people will take the opportunity to move away from some of the uglier, more overcrowded places on our planet."[3]

The advancement of technology has transferred a never before seen freedom to humanity—the freedom to earn a living regardless of one's geographical and physical location. The spread of social networking sites like "Facebook" and the development of the internet have enabled people to exchange ideas and knowledge irrespective of country of origin or social standing. This unparalleled international interaction has given rise to a new international movement towards universal democracy and transparency – a movement being led by Digital Nomads, New Independent Problem-Solvers or the Creative Class.

---

[3] Makimoto, Tsugio; Manners, David, Digital Nomad, pg 22

A New Independent Problem-Solver/ Creative Class

In 2002, Richard Florida, a professor at Carnegie-Mellon University in Pittsburgh, Pennsylvania, published a book explaining his research and findings on the mobility of a group of people he terms the Creative Class. His research concentrated on statistical evidence available to him from the United States of America although he touched upon the fact that his newly termed class of people exist worldwide and that their characteristics are similar if not identical worldwide.

People in this new class are creative professionals with a great earning potential, not entirely unlike the Digital Nomads examined by Tsugio Makimoto & David Manners, and the rise of this class is directly related to the growing need for and acknowledgement of innovation and creativity as a saleable good. "The economic need for creativity has registered itself in the rise of a new class...Some 38 million Americans, 30 percent of all employed people, belong to this new class. I define the core of the Creative Class to include people in science and engineering, architecture and design, education, arts, music and entertainment, whose economic function is to create new ideas, new technology and/or new creative content."[4]

Although parallels between the theories of Makimoto, Manners and Florida exist, Dr. Florida chooses to distance himself from the ideas of those researchers whom he calls techno-futurists by emphasizing the fact that his research shows that

---

[4] Florida, Richard, The Rise of the Creative Class, pg. 8

quality of place is a decisive factor in the choice of residence of his Creative Class. "In contrast to the many techno-futurists who say the wired and wireless information age has made location and community irrelevant, the creative workers I talk with say they are vitally important. These people insist they need to live in places that offer stimulating, creative environments. Many will not even consider taking jobs in certain cities or regions...", and further, "I also meet Creative Class people who use location as their primary criterion in a proactive sense: They will pick a place they want to live, then focus their job search there."[5]

These ideas do not contradict those of Makimoto and Manners. In fact, through the increase in wealth and the increase in mobility generated by the rise in the need for creativity, precisely the result that Makimoto and Manners predicted has come true. People in this new group, the Creative Class, according to Dr. Florida, are actively choosing their place of residence and bringing with them all of the inherent qualities of their class.

Additionally, should their needs not be met by their initially chosen place, these people have no qualms packing their belongings and moving again. A number of notable artists, musicians and authors such as Shania Twain, Tina Turner and Donna Leon have chosen to leave their home countries to move to other places which offer them the quality of life that they are seeking.

This loss of deep roots and strong ties to a community, a definitive change from the basic values

---

[5] Florida, Richard, The Rise of the Creative Class, pg. 95

of the post-WWII generation, is almost entirely due to a change in the economic structure of the industrialized nations. Gone are the days when a person could expect to stay with one company his or her entire life and long gone are the days when a highly qualified independent problem-solving person would choose to.

"Still, many people have the option of a stable, secure job and yet choose to leave—whether by job-hopping or by going solo. In doing so they often resist pay raises or other efforts to retain them. What really motivates these people? Certainly part of the story lies in the demise of the old social contract: As companies began to breach it, people felt less inclined to keep their end...Or as Stanford's Pfeffer likes to say: Loyalty isn't dead. Companies have driven it away."[6]

The benefit of this new work environment for companies is also obvious. Companies no longer feel a moral obligation to their employees. Terminating employees has become purely an economic calculation. "In fact some companies have reduced costs by terminating employees and then promptly hiring them back as independent contractors. The company no longer has to provide benefits, and doesn't have to promise, even implicitly, continued employment once a project is done."[7] This transformation in the working environment was a gradual one in the United States, which is only now beginning to understand the ramifications of it.

---

[6] Florida, Richard, The Rise of the Creative Class, pp. 109-110
[7] ibid., pg. 110

In Europe the process of transformation of the job market is only now beginning, allowing clever governments to begin a process of adjustment long before reaching the critical stage. The trend researcher Matthias Horx from Germany has already documented the coming change facing Europe: "The world is changing. Work is no longer a lifelong repetition of the same things; it's becoming more creative, also more stressful. People are getting older. Therefore we are going to have a different job and work structure in the future information age, also different social contracts and social systems. This change is possible, as other countries have shown us (translation author)."[8]

But what is powering the rise in the number of these creative people and their Creative Class and what makes these people so special? "Many social scientists claim that we are living in an economy powered by information, information technology and the knowledge transferred through this technology. However, this is only partially correct. Many say that we now live in an 'information' economy or a 'knowledge' economy. But what's more fundamentally true is that we now have an economy powered by human creativity. Creativity...is now the *decisive* source of competitive advantage. In virtually every industry, from automobiles to fashion, food products, and information technology itself, the winners in the long

[8] Wientjes, Bernd: Alles in allem: Rosige Aussichten – TV Interview mit dem Zukunftsforscher Matthias Horx: Warum den Deutschen vor der Zukunft nicht bange sein muss, Trierischer Volksfreund, Nr. 303, Silvester 2003, Themen der Zeit: Wissenschaft, Seite 3

run are those who can create and keep creating. This has always been true, from the days of the Agricultural Revolution to the Industrial Revolution. But in the past few decades we've come to recognize it clearly and act upon it systematically."[9]

So the recognition within the business community of the need for creativity as a competitive advantage has fueled the growth of the number of workers who earn their living being creative, that is, producing creative solutions to problems. This is in huge contrast to other types of workers, such as the service and industrial or working class workers. "Those in the Working Class and the Service Class are primarily paid to execute according to plan, while those in the Creative Class are primarily paid to create and have considerably more autonomy and flexibility than the other two classes to do so."[10]

Creative people, searching for creative solutions to increasingly difficult problems, are therefore the backbone of the business community and decisive to the future economic conditions of countries and their governments. "The winners in the global job market are the new highly motivated, cosmopolitically orientated achievers. These are people who are paid for the identification of problems; for developing strategies to solve the problems; and who are paid to solve the problems themselves. Employees for routine work or for routine services are easy to find in the global job market. For this group of people, the future looks increasingly unfavorable. Uneducated

---

[9] Florida, Richard, The Rise of the Creative Class, pg. 5
[10] ibid., pg. 8

24

and unqualified workers will have few opportunities (translation author)."[11]

These highly creative people are so important for the future of companies that they have caused the methodology which some companies apply to decide where they should locate their businesses to significantly change. "Robert Nunn, the CEO of ADD Semiconductor said that 'the key element of building a technology business is attracting the right people to the company. It's a combination of experience, skill set, raw intelligence, and energy. The most important thing is to be somewhere where you have a pool of people to draw that from.'"[12]

Some companies still consider it important to locate to a place where they can receive large government tax incentives or where the infrastructure is built to their specifications. Other more savvy companies are increasingly foregoing the opportunity to reap huge tax rewards and are settling in places where they receive no government support whatsoever, but where they have a large employment population of highly creative people to choose from. "Access to talented and creative people is to modern business what access to coal and iron ore was to steelmaking. It determines where companies will choose to locate and grow, and this in turn changes the ways cities must compete. As Hewlett-Packard's CEO, Carley Fiorina, once told this

---

[11] Oberweis, Marcel, Vernetztes Denken statt Fachwissen pur, Luxemburger Wort, January 17, 2004, Le marché national de l'emploi au Grand-Duché de Luxembourg, pg. 1

[12] Loftus, Peter, "Location, Location, Location", The Wall Street Journal, October 15, 2001, pg. R14

nation's (USA) governors: 'Keep your tax incentives and highway interchanges; we will go where the highly skilled people are.'"[13]

Contrary to past schemes of business development, the trend has now become one in which innovative technologies, venture capital and then companies themselves have become mobile, moving to find knowledge workers instead of knowledge workers moving to the companies. "In a curious reversal, instead of people moving to jobs, I was finding that companies were moving to or forming in places that had the skilled *people*."[14]

These highly skilled and creative people, for their part, are no longer tying themselves to any one company, but are taking more responsibility for their own résumés and are increasingly "playing the field" in terms of work. "The most notable feature of the new labor market, as just about every one agrees, is that people don't stay tied to companies anymore. Instead of moving up through the ranks of one organization, they move laterally from company to company in search of what they want. The playing field is horizontal and people are always on the roll."[15] As mentioned above, this is in part due to the fact that the work environment has become increasingly unstable for the worker. Companies feel no moral obligation towards their workers; therefore the workers no longer feel a moral obligation towards their employer or even more importantly towards their home countries or home cities.

---

[13] Florida, Richard, The Rise of the Creative Class, pg. 6
[14] ibid., pg. x
[15] ibid., pg. 104

Additionally, the worker cannot count on long-term security; therefore the worker no longer desires it. The resulting effect of this is that workers will try to create their own security. These workers tire of the corporate environment and the politicing which is part of that environment. "Those in smaller, entrepreneurial companies grow tired of the stress and the management-by-chaos. People in both settings tire of worrying about losing their jobs."[16] This causes them to seek options for remaining self-employed or at least retaining the lion share of control over their occupational destinies.

The new creative economy has created a need for creative workers. These creative workers, well aware of their market value, no longer choose to be tied to any given company and are moving laterally within the job market as they feel a need to. Additionally, they are also moving from one geographical location to another as they feel compelled to. "...The vertical hierarchy and traditional career ladders have been replaced by a horizontal division of labor, sideways career moves between companies and a horizontal labor market."[17]

The second aspect of this new creative economy is a change in the point of reference of these new independent problem solvers. These problem solvers have now come to identify themselves more with a profession or occupation than a company. "This is partly the product of the move to domain-specific knowledge...people (are) increasingly defining themselves both by the creative content of their work

---

[16] Florida, Richard, The Rise of the Creative Class, pg. 110
[17] ibid., pg. 114

and by their lifestyle interests: biker, climber, and musician. In search of greater challenge, autonomy or satisfaction, people once again tend to move horizontally rather than vertically."[18]

Finally, these new independent problem solving workers are actively taking responsibility for the development of their careers through further training and education. Where, in the past, the company could be counted on to train individuals so that they could progress up the corporate ladder, the new business reality requires individuals to actively seek out and plan their own career development. "(They) not only assume the risks of job moves, (they) assume the task of taking care of their creativity—investing in it, supporting it and nurturing it. For instance, creative workers spend tremendous amounts of time and money on education. They go through basic port-of-entry education, education for a career-track change, and ongoing learning and upgrading of skills."[19]

The motivation for frequent job changes, career path changes and even changes of residential location are numerous. Prime among the reason for these changes is a general dissatisfaction with the way in which companies are organized and managed. In the past workers would accept the corporate hierarchy and structure as a given. The new independent problem-solving worker, however, is no longer accepting this as a necessary way of life. "It's management—inconsistent, incompetent or capricious. A big complaint is that management doesn't "get it" or

---

[18] Florida, Richard, The Rise of the Creative Class, pg. 114
[19] ibid.

fails to appreciate employee efforts. Even worse are major changes of direction that cause employees to think that all of their hard work has been for naught. This will drive even the most loyal of employees to abandon ship."[20]

This is a decided shift from the motivations of past generations of workers, where the primary motivating factor in taking and holding a position was the size of the salary and the additional benefits received. The problem-solving generation of workers wants more. Not only is the size of the salary important, but the moral fiber of the company or organization, the management style and a host of other "soft" factors play a part in attracting and maintaining these workers.

Therefore there seems to be: "an inter-generational shift from emphasis on economic and physical security toward increasing emphasis on self-expression, subjective well-being, and quality of life...This cultural shift is found throughout advanced industrial societies; it seems to emerge among birth cohorts that have grown up under conditions in which survival is taken for granted."[21]

The people of this new independent problem-solving generation are pursuing personal values and are fulfilling their own personal desires and needs. The work of the Nobel Prize winning economist Robert Fogel gives support to this noted shift in the work ethic of this group of workers. In his book The Fourth Great Awakening, Robert Fogel examines the changes happening to the highly industrialized

[20] Florida, Richard, The Rise of the Creative Class, pg. 111
[21] Inglehart, Ronald, "Culture and Democracy", pg. 84

nations and maintains that there will be a shift in the motivation of a growing segment of the population towards their work.

In the future, so Fogel states, a growing portion of the population will work for the challenge of a position, the enjoyment associated with their occupation, for the chance to do good, for the opportunity to make a contribution towards society, and for an opportunity to learn and further develop their skills. He suggests that ultimately these motivations will outweigh other factors such as compensation as the main motivator for taking on a position. Richard Florida, within the body of his works, maintains that this change has already taken place.

Essentially, these members of society are "self-actualizing" to use a phrase coined by Abraham Maslow, whose theories will be examined at length in the next chapter. Maslow's theories were often cited and quoted by Richard Florida in his works. Florida even acknowledged the connection of his theory with the work of Dr. Maslow when he claimed that "creative workers do not merely move up the scale in Abraham Maslow's classic hierarchy of needs. Most are not very worried about meeting the basic needs of subsistence; they're already on the upper rungs of the ladder, where intrinsic rewards such as esteem and self-actualization are sought. And having reached the high end, they can and do move laterally from seeking one form of esteem or actualization to another."[22]

Having a growing number of members of society belonging to this independent problem-solving

[22] Florida, Richard, The Rise of the Creative Class, pg. 101

group means that the society in question has provided a structure which insures the continued fulfillment of the lower human needs, on the pyramid of needs, thereby freeing up members of society to pursue higher goals. A notable lack in the number of these members of society will indicate a lack in provision of the lower needs necessary to insure a healthy society.

What is the motivation for implementing changes to the structure of a company, or city, or on the highest level country in order to attract and keep these independent problem-solving workers?

Many notable scientists have already examined aspects of this issue, among them, Jeffrey Pfeffer from Stanford University. Writing in an article for a corporate management magazine he asserted that companies could be expected to receive a considerable performance payback if they managed these workers well. "All that separates you from your competitors are the skills, knowledge, commitment and abilities of the people who work for you. There is a very compelling business case for this idea: Companies that manage people right will outperform companies that don't by 30 percent to 40 percent."[23] For a society, the reward of keeping its creative people is a booming economy and success in worldwide competition. In the long term, the reward of keeping the independent problem solving societal members is a sustainable future.

In a specific example: Currently, the German government has started its second push, in approx-

[23] Pfeffer, Jeffrey, „Danger: Toxic Company", Fast Company, November 19, 1998, pg 152

imately 10 years, to attract foreign creative problem-solving workers to the country. Industries in Germany are suffering from a perceived lack of highly-educated problem-solvers and have compelled the government to examine its immigration policies as a result. Without these workers, so the argumentation of the industry, they cannot develop new markets or maintain the advancements that they have already achieved. The situation is said to be dire.

On the other hand, Germany has one of the highest university enrollment percentages in the European Union. The problem, therefore, is not one of not being able to produce these creative workers; the problem in Germany is that the country, through its political policies and treatment of its citizens, is not able to keep them. According to a 2010 study by the Bundesinstitut für Bevölkerungsforschung the number of emigrants from Germany has increased dramatically rising from 50,000 in the 1970's to 155,000 in 2009. Furthermore, half of these German citizens had at least an undergraduate degree. The most interesting fact stemming from this study, however, was that although the majority of academics that left Germany eventually returned, the percentage of management or those that held leadership positions ultimately returning to Germany was significantly smaller.[24] This means that although the educated workers might eventually return to the country, the innovators are most certain *not* to want to return.

Creative people look for very specific things in a company, city and country with which they choose

---

[24] Ette, Andreas; Sauer, Lenore, "Abschied von Einwanderungsland Deutschland?", pp. 6-7

to be associated. According to Richard Florida they have a strong motivation to be associated with organizations and to be part of environments that allow them the freedom that they need to be creative. Additionally, they need places that "value their input, challenge them, have mechanisms for mobilizing resources around ideas and are receptive to both small changes and the occasional big idea. Companies and places that can provide this kind of environment, regardless of size, will have an edge in attracting, managing and motivating creative talent. The same companies and places will also tend to enjoy a flow of innovation, reaping competitive advantage in the short run and evolutionary advantage in the long run."[25] Also, one does not need to be overly attuned to the needs of the Creative Class to realize that "while certain environments promote creativity, others can most certainly kill it."[26]

Creative people have different values than their post-WWII parents did. This is in large part due to the fact that this generation, in the past, has not faced the same levels of scarcity or shortage that that generation did. Those societies which have not yet attained a general level of guaranteed subsistence (and former generations of the developed world) work simply to survive. This drive toward subsistence ties up creative energy and does not allow the further development of new ideas and innovations. Guaranteed basic subsistence and the "rise of an affluent or 'post-scarcity' economy" provides the opportunity to invest wealth, time and

[25] Florida, Richard, The Rise of the Creative Class, pg. 40
[26] ibid.

personal talents in enjoying other aspects of life and therefore provides further choices and personal freedoms. "Precisely because they attained high levels of economic security the Western societies that were the first to industrialize have gradually come to emphasize post-materialist values, giving higher priority to the quality of life than to economic growth."[27]

Ronald Inglehart, for his part, also acknowledged a debt to the theories of Dr. Abraham Maslow when he explained that: "the complementary concept of a need hierarchy (Maslow, 1954) helped shape the survey items used to measure value priorities. In its simplest form, the idea of a need hierarchy would probably command almost universal assent. The fact that unmet physiological needs take priority over social, intellectual, or aesthetic needs has been demonstrated all too often in human history: starving people will go to almost any length to obtain food. The rank ordering of human needs varies as we move beyond those needs directly related to survival...But there does seem to be a basic distinction between the "material" needs for physiological sustenance and safety, and non-physiological needs such as those for esteem, self-expression, and aesthetic satisfaction."[28]

Additionally, a universally high-level of tolerance and a dislike for mediocrity are among the characteristics of the members of this new independent problem-solving or creative class. According to

---

[27] Inglehart, Ronald, "Globalization and Postmodern Values", pg. 225

[28] ibid., pg. 33

34

Inglehart's research, places that demonstrate an increase in lifestyle issues, such as the United States and in most European societies, also display an expansion in tolerance of other groups and a support of gender equality.

Florida, for his part, states that these values are reflected in his Creative Class. Furthermore, Inglehart discovered a general movement away from traditional norms and values toward more progressive ones and the tendency that the larger the economies grow and the more living standards improve, the less people are attached to large institutions and the more they become open and tolerant towards differing views with respect to personal relationships.

Inglehart also specifically examined the characteristics of Europe's Creative Class or Postmodernizational members, building upon the 1981 European Values Systems Survey directed by Jan Kerkhofs, Ruud de Moor, Joan Linz, Elisabeth Noelle-Neumann, Jacques-Rene Rabier and Helene Riffault as well as upon the Euro-Barometer surveys directed by Karl-Heinz Reif and Anna Melich of the Commission of the European Union[29]. Through his research, Inglehart found that although there were notable differences between the European countries in terms of values, the majority of those countries were beyond the point of modernization and squarely in the middle of postmodernization.

The modernization theorists argue:

"that a broad syndrome of changes has been linked with modern economic development.

---

[29] Inglehart, Ronald, "Globalization and Postmodern Values", pg. ix

These changes include urbanization, industrialization, occupational specialization, mass formal education, development of mass media, secularization, individuation, the rise of entrepreneurs and entrepreneurial motivations, bureaucratization, the mass production assembly line, and the emergence of the modern state. The material core of this process is industrialization; and though the industrial revolution originated in the West, this process is not inherently Western and should not be confused with Westernization. Although there are arguments about what the "real" driving force is behind this syndrome, there is widespread agreement that these changes include technological, economic, cultural, and political components."[30]

Clearly, the majority of Western European countries have long past this point of economic development, although one can argue as to the degree in which these countries had success in the process.

Postmodernization, however, brings with it an ultimate shift in values. Inglehart discovered that the emphasis in a Postmodern society is on the individual and the individuals perceived needs; which correlates with the findings of Florida, with the idea of the Digital Nomad and ultimately with the theories of Abraham Maslow. "In Postmodernization, the core project is to maximize individual well-being, which is increasingly dependent on subjective

[30] Inglehart, Ronald, Modernization and Postmodernization, pg. 70

factors. Human behavior shifts from being dominated by the economic imperatives of providing food, clothing, and shelter toward the pursuit of quality of life concerns. Even economic behavior becomes less a matter of meeting the survival needs and becomes increasingly oriented toward attaining subjective well being."[31]

In Figure 1, the comparison between the inherent values of the three societal forms shows the gradual change from collective values to individual values. In

	Traditional	*Modern*	*Postmodern*
Core Societal Project	Survival in a steady-state economy	Maximize economic growth	Maximize subjective well-being
Individual Values	Traditional religious and communal norms	Achievement motivation	Post-materialist and Postmodern values
Authority System	Traditional authority	Rational legal authority	De-emphasis of both legal and religious authority

Figure 1. Traditional, Modern, and Postmodern Society: Societal Goals and Individual Needs   Source: Inglehart, Ronald

many, if not all, of the European nations, a marked tendency toward the Postmodern values can be documented. The documented shift in the values of the European nations from the Modern values toward the Postmodern values can be traced back to a long continuous period of economic prosperity without a direct threat to security or stability. This has been the case in the industrialized nations of

---

[31] Inglehart, Ronald, Modernization and Postmodernization, pg. 76

Europe, as it has been in the United States and other developed nations, since the end of WWII.

As Inglehart argues, a yearly increase in the percentage of citizens holding these values can be linked to the intergenerational exchange of values due to the natural replacement of older generational members. Not surprising, the World Values Survey also discovered a direct correlation between income levels and the rate of subjective well-being documented by the survey subjects. It could be noted, between countries of large economic differences, that the inhabitants of wealthier countries showed a markedly higher rate of subjective well-being than the poorer countries.

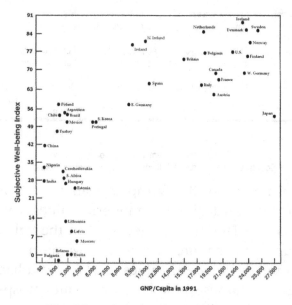

Figure 2. Economic development and subjective well-being
Source: Inglehart, Ronald, Modernization and Postmodernization, pg. 62

In figure 2, the survey results of the 1991 World Values Survey are graphically depicted. The relationship between GNP/ Capita in 1991 and the index of Subjective Well-Being is clearly shown. "The relationship between economic development level and subjective well-being is remarkably strong and is significant at the .00001 level...Furthermore, the linkage between economic level and subjective well-being manifests itself not only at the cross-national level but also within given societies: as common sense might lead one to expect, people with high incomes tend to have higher levels of subjective well-being than those with low incomes. Moreover, Eastern and Western Germany provide a sort of controlled experiment, in which nationality and culture are held constant, but in Eastern Germany, per capita income is much lower than in Western Germany: as our interpretation implies, the Western Germans show substantially higher levels of subjective well-being than do the Eastern Germans...this same comparison helps explain why the impact of economic development eventually levels off: in terms of what they consider important, economic factors (such as income) rank much higher among Eastern Germans than among Western Germans; and conversely, noneconomic aspects of life (such as leisure time) are considered much more important by the Western Germans than by the Eastern Germans (Statistisches Bundesamt, 1994: 441)."[32]

Despite a clear correlation between income levels and rate of subjective well-being between countries of differing standards of living; Dr. Inglehart discovered that the correlation ceased to exist once a certain

---

[32] Inglehart, Ronald, Modernization and Postmodernization, pg. 63

threshold of economic development was crossed. After crossing that threshold, the major source of difference in the level of subjective well-being was found in lifestyle issues. "Within wealthy societies, the correlation between income and subjective well-being is relatively weak. In societies where a higher income may make the difference between survival and starvation, a good income is a pretty good first approximation of what well-being really means. But in rich societies, income differences have a surprisingly small impact on subjective well-being..."[33]

Additionally: "the overall evidence supports the thesis of diminishing marginal utility from economic gains. As figure 2 suggests, the transition from a society of scarcity to a society of security brings a dramatic increase in subjective well-being. But (at roughly the economic level of Ireland in 1990) we find a threshold at which economic growth no longer seems to increase subjective well-being significantly. This may be linked with the fact that at this level starvation is no longer a real concern for most people. Survival begins to be taken for granted. Significant numbers of Post-materialists begin to emerge, and for them further economic gains no longer produce an increase in subjective well-being. Beyond this level, economic development no longer seems to bring rising subjective well-being. The stage is set for the Postmodern shift to begin."[34]

So, if we follow the theory of Dr. Inglehart, the society which seeks to create an environment in

---

[33] Inglehart, Ronald, Modernization and Postmodernization, pg. 64
[34] ibid.
40

which the majority of its citizens have a significant sense of well-being, must focus its efforts on improving the social needs spectrum most necessary for the further development of its citizens. In places in which the survival issue is most predominant, the society must concentrate its efforts on improving economic conditions.

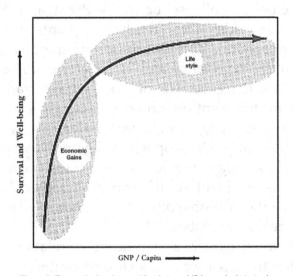

Figure 3. Economic development leads to a shift in survival strategies
Source: Inglehart, Ronald, Modernization and Postmodernization, pg. 65

However, once a certain level of economic and social standard is reached, the development efforts must focus on improving quality of life standards within the society. It is also possible, as Dr. Inglehart suggests, that a mix of values exists in the same context. An adequate solution to the development issues of such a society would include the support of both economic and quality of life improvements, in a mixture deemed by the particular circumstances.

"At low levels of economic development, even modest economic gains bring a high return in terms

41

of caloric intake, clothing, shelter, medical care, and ultimately in life expectancy itself. For individuals to give top priority to maximizing economic gains, and for a society to give top priority to economic growth, is a highly effective survival strategy. But once a society has reached a certain threshold of development—at about the level where the Soviet Union was before its collapse, or where Portugal or South Korea are today—one reaches a point at which further economic growth brings only minimal gains in both life expectancy and in subjective well-being. There is still a good deal of cross-national variation, but from this point on, non-economic aspects of life become increasingly important influences on how long, and how well, people live. Beyond this point, a rational strategy would be to place increasing emphasis on quality-of-life concerns, rather than to continue the inflexible pursuit of economic growth as if it were a good in itself."[35]

As noted earlier: a significant correlation exists between the Creative Class citizens touted by Richard Florida; the Digital Nomads extolled by Tsugio and Manners; the Postmodernist favored by Inglehart; the self-actualizing person supported by Maslow and the New Independent Problem Solvers championed by this author. We have also seen that all of these citizens play a decisive role in shaping their surroundings, if only through their creative potential, their sizable income and the economic impact that it has on their communities.

---

[35] Inglehart, Ronald, Modernization and Postmodernization, pp. 64-65

Additionally, once enough of these people have gathered in one place, a tipping point is reached and their values become the dominant ones. This, in turn, then has an affect on every aspect of the society. In industrialized nations it is increasingly becoming clear that the significant qualities distinguishing one society or community from another are lifestyle qualities. At a certain level of economic development, this is the major differing factor. The question then becomes what the qualities are that these people are looking for in the community of their choice? Which are the features that makes them seek to choose one specific location over another?

These new independent problem-solving workers are primarily looking for aspects which give them a certain level of quality of life which also include a quality of the work environment: "The company is excellent, he told me. It has terrific people and the work is challenging. But the clincher was: 'It's in Austin!' 'Why is that good?' I asked. There are lots of young people, he explained, and a tremendous amount to do, a thriving music scene, ethnic and cultural diversity, fabulous outdoor recreation, and great nightlife...What's more, Austin is affordable, unlike Silicon Valley, another place that offered the kinds of work he desired...'I can have a life in Austin,' he concluded, 'not merely a job.'"[36]

Based upon the observations of Richard Florida, the Creative Class requires the following amenities in an environment in which they choose to live and work:

---

[36] Florida, Richard, The Rise of the Creative Class, pg. 217

- **Thick Labor Markets**: Thick labor markets provide multitudes of opportunities to find exactly the opportunity that they need or want in order to become creative as well as the freedom to change places of employment if they are no longer happy and satisfied with their current situation.
- **Proximity to nature**: Nature allows creative people to recharge their batteries.
- **Nightlife**: A vibrant nightlife provides opportunities to develop new ideas both directly and through new experiences. A multitude of options provides needed input in order to generate creative solutions to problems and is seen as a sign that a city or society understands the needs of creative people.
- **Social Interaction**: A strong social network and the opportunity to develop one offsets the lack of an inherent social network and replaces the traditional ones because these creative workers are more likely to be single, live alone and change jobs as well as cities/countries more often.
- **Diversity**: Diversity of nationalities, ethnic groups, races, ages, languages and alternative appearances provide extra food for the creative problem-solving process. A mix of influences provides a rich base upon which to draw solutions from.
- **Authenticity**: A place chosen must be a place that is "real". It must have a history, a development and a flair that is unique and

singular in comparison with other places. It must be a place that is easily recognizable. This authenticity of place is a result of many factors including the built environment, the people who live and work there and the music which is produced in the place. This is called an "audio identity". Once again authenticity, uniqueness, singularity and "realness" provide a source from which creative solutions are drawn.

- **Identity**: It must have a recognizable identity. This is because a highly mobile and flexible workforce requires an alternative anchor. This anchor is provided through the status of place. In the past, workers were primarily marked and recognizable through the notoriety of their workplace. Today, the notoriety of international companies has been replaced by the notoriety of the place of residence. A place that conveys a high level of status is therefore more likely to attract these workers.[37]

These requirement of place factors were compiled based upon general observations. These were noted by Richard Florida during his research into the Creative Class. As different as they may seem at first glance, they do exhibit certain unifying characteristics. These features display certain underlying values and traits of these individuals and can be summed up in the following manner:

---

[37] Florida, Richard, The Rise of the Creative Class, pp. 223-230

"Generally, one can think of quality of place as having three dimensions:
- What's there: the combination of the built environment and the natural environment; a proper setting for pursuit of creative lives.
- Who's there: the diverse kinds of people, interacting and providing cues that anyone can plug into and make a life in that community.
- What's going on: the vibrancy of street life, café culture, arts, music and people engaging in outdoor activities—altogether a lot of active, exciting, creative endeavors."[38]

These characteristics play a large part in determining if a member of the Creative Class feels at home in his surroundings. This, in turn, will also feature in any future decisions made as to whether to remain in any particular location or not. Ultimately, the quality of life aspects of any environment will establish if these important societal members flourish.

The qualities of place mentioned above are aspects being sought by this new and increasingly dominant group of citizens called the Creative Class or Independent Problem-Solvers. Through the importance of their role in society, their needs and wishes are being integrated into planning and development concepts which, when implemented, combine to create an environment conducive to creative thought and output and sets the stage for economic growth and stability.

---

[38] Florida, Richard, The Rise of the Creative Class, pp. 231-232

The Global Citizen

The growth in the number of new independent problem-solving workers has created a market for experiences. Drawing upon the fact that creative workers require both diversity in their environments as well as diverse life experiences (in order to form the experience base from which they draw their creative solutions), marketers worldwide have discovered a tremendous consumer base to which they can sell these events.

The boom in worldwide travel of the 1980's and 1990's, which held on until the events of 2001 and the general market degeneration of 2008 and 2009 dampened the surge for a short while, documented the worldwide need for creative experiences. Although the events of those years changed the scope of travel for a time and created a revival in national travel as opposed to international travel; the need for creative experiences could not be stemmed.

Author, Elizabeth Kruempelmann, documented this worldwide desire for creative experiences in her book, The Global Citizen: "the traditional rules of living and working have changed for good. The world is becoming more flexible to fit our more demanding lifestyles...Despite the innovative technology that makes life easier and more mobile, for many of you the missing piece of a "perfect" life puzzle is living, working, and traveling abroad...The mystery and excitement of what lies beyond the familiar borders has captivated our imagination since the beginning of time—this phenomenon is nothing new. What is new, however, is that it is finally your turn in the cosmic cycle of things to strike out and discover countries, people, languages, ways of doing business, and many other aspects of life that are the current state of affairs in the world...now is the time to gather your creative juices and make it happen."[39]

In addition to a growth in international experience travel, a growing number of citizens also expand upon their base of life-experiences by crossing international lines to become residents of other countries. This creates an interesting scenario. Lacking the traditional ties to their home countries, these Global Citizens or new independent problem-solving members of society are potential residents of any city or any country in the world. "This book (The Global Citizen) is unique in that it expands on the new emphasis many people are putting on the integration of international experience into their lifelong personal and professional goals. It focuses on a common desire to experience the world in a meaningful way through educational travel, academic learning, volunteering, or professional experience overseas. Not only is international exposure desired by students, professionals, families, and retirees, but it is also establishing itself as the new threshold for career success and life-long development."[40] Expanding personal growth experiences is the major motivational factor driving these people.

The United States Government has also acknowledged an increase in international competition for the best and the brightest. "As other nations become more attractive to mobile immigrant talent, America is becoming less so. A recent study by the National Science Board found that the U.S. government issued

---

[39] Kruempelmann, Elizabeth, The Global Citizen, pg. xi
[40] ibid., pg. xiv

74,000 visas for immigrants to work in science and technology in 2002, down from 166,000 in 2001–an astonishing drop of 55 percent. This is matched by similar, though smaller-scale, declines in other categories of talented immigrants, from finance experts to entertainers. Part of this contraction is derived from what we hope are short-term security concerns–as federal agencies have restricted visas from certain countries after September 11, (2001). More disturbingly, we find indications that fewer educated foreigners are choosing to come to the United States. For instance, most of the decline in science and technology immigrants in the National Science Board study was due to a drop in applications."[41] It is astonishing, that the US still believes that it only has to convince talent living outside the US to immigrate. The problem in the US, however, is an even deeper one. Many talented US citizens are beginning to turn their back on their home country never to return.

This is a source of real long-term concern, because, with their strong economic potential, these people are also among the most desirable of the potential residents of a city or a country. They are, however, also among the most demanding of potential residents. "So, what is the Global Citizen anyway? Global citizens are global-minded people like you and (I) who crave international experience and are passionate about living fulfilled lives. The term "global citizen" creates awareness of a whole category of internationally oriented people who

---

[41] Florida, Richard, "Creative Class War", Washington Monthly, January 15, 2004, Online: www.alternet.org

derive satisfaction from life by discovering the world...By living in foreign countries; global citizens tend to form a unique cross-cultural group. Their worldly outlook on life bonds them together with like-minded thinkers who appreciate the world at large—its people, cultures, history, engineering marvels, natural resources, and all the fascinating facets of life that make the world an exciting place. The global citizen's philosophy is based on the awareness that stimulating experiences of living in foreign countries help us develop as people. As we clarify our understanding of ourselves and our world, we improve the quality of our lives."[42]

This quotation is well worth keeping in mind, because it describes the inner motivation of an increasingly important segment of society. These people, whether termed Digital Nomads, Cultural Creatives, Creative Class, Global Citizens, Postmodernist members of society or Independent Problem-Solvers are the driving factor in a social revolution which is beginning to manifest itself and will continue to grow with ever-increasing strength until it radically transforms every aspect of our present society.

However logical this postulation is, it does still have its detractors. These cynics, in large part, have concentrated their focus on one particular person purporting these ideas. Bearing the lion's share of the criticism is the author and creator of the term Creative Class, Dr. Richard Florida.

---

[42] Kruempelmann, Elizabeth, The Global Citizen, pg. 1

Why I Don't Love Richard Florida[43]

Dr. Richard Florida is a very controversial person. Within the United States he is a leading pop economist and quoted, cited and invited regularly by the media. Within the planning community at large he is generally loved by certain types of US builders and developers, while at the same time being hated with an increasing passion by most European urban planners and some of his own colleagues within the United States. The question begs to be asked, how can a singular human being invoke such opposing feelings and opinions?

The answer becomes apparent when one takes a look at the controversy through the eyes of human nature. Fact is: Richard Florida was not the first person to highlight the growing importance of human capital and human creativity in the future development of societies. Beginning with the Digital Nomads, this idea can be traced back to many noted and not so famous societal thinkers like: Paul H. Ray with his Cultural Creatives; Charles Landry and his Creative City; Robert Fogel and his Fourth Great Awakening; Hazel Henderson with her Win-Win-World; Mickey Kaus and his End of Equality; Elizabeth Kruempelmann with her Global Citizens; John Howkins with his Creative Economy, and many more. All of these ideas pre-date or emerged at the same time as Richard Florida's controversial book. The Rise of the Creative Class.

"Florida has come along to codify and capture a movement already in progress."[44]

[43] Jacobs, Karrie, http://www.metropolismag.com/story/20050222/why-i-dont-love-richard-florida, Feb. 22, 2005

If all of these professionals said the same thing or had similar ideas, why the witch-hunt against Florida? This is where human nature comes into play. Dr. Richard Florida had the brilliant idea to name these highly-educated, independent problem-solvers **"a CLASS"**, to paraphrase other colleagues, add some own ideas, and then to package those words in a pleasing form. By choosing the term "class" he deliberately chose a word laced with societal baggage—most of it bad, all of it controversial—which then guaranteed that his book would become controversial. He then made a cardinal mistake in the realm of academics—**HE MADE MONEY! Lots of it!**

Researchers, so typically thought, are not supposed to become wealthy off of their studies. By some strange twist in logic, if one earns money off of research, it loses its purity. Academics are supposed to be grey-haired, slightly disheveled, slightly absent-minded but never, **never**, rich. They should be purists that leave the "dirty" job of making money through that research to the business people. "Pure academics" and "pure science" should *never* be dirtied with money so the opinion of the greatest majority of academics. Thus the oldest human emotion— enviousness—comes into play.

A clear example of this was heard on the Chicago Public Radio broadcast "Eight Forty-Eight". In an interview with Robert Bruegmann, professor of Art History, Architecture and Urban Planning at the University of Illinois at Chicago and author of Sprawl: A Compact History, when asked at length about his

[44] Jacobs, Karrie, http://www.metropolismag.com/story/ 20050222/why-i-dont-love-richard-florida, Feb. 22, 2005

opinion of Richard Florida's work, Bruegmann answered, "He **certainly** has made a lot of money off of that singular idea."[45]

But in all fairness to the critics of Richard Florida, there are a few points of critique worth mentioning here. First of all, in contrast to other colleagues, Florida claimed that his Creative Class could be documented within a society by examining the gay population of a society. Once again, Florida chose a highly charged segment of society to prove his point. Also, Dr. Florida initially claimed that certain professions formed the basis for his "class". These occupations included, among others: media designers, fashion designers, architects, artists and other "creative" work. This became a great bone of contention for many critics, prompting them to state that many occupations are creative and everyone could be creative within their own occupations.

True as this may be, it misses the point. Florida made this selection as a way to statistically test his hypothesis. To prove his ideas it was necessary to make some choices, so he chose gays and certain professions. Later he internalized the criticism and began to openly state that there were Creative Class members to be found in every occupation. Ironically both Florida and his critics are right—**and wrong**.

Independent problem-solvers cannot be organized according to occupations or sexual preference, although certain groups and fields of work tend to attract them. The reality is that these societal mem-

---

[45] Cuddy, Alison with Bruegmann, Robert, Chicago Public Radio, Eight Forty-Eight: "The Case for Success in the Suburbs", Broadcast: March 3rd, 2009 – 20:00

bers **do** exist, but they exist in all realms of society and within all social groups and professions. This is because independent problem-solvers become independent problem-solvers primarily in two ways.

Firstly, as a result of specific external living conditions. These conditions provide them with the environment necessary to move through an inner psychological or spiritual progression. The provision of a social structure in which the basic human needs of food, clothing and shelter are met; where the economic gains of provision are amply protected; where the person feels like he or she is part of a group and included in society; and where the person achieves a certain level of recognition for his labors, will lead to a change in thought processes and ultimately help the person to develop into the best individual that they can be. This is by far the most common way.

The second possible way of becoming an independent problem solver is essentially the inverse of the first. Here the individual sets off on a course to achieve psychological or spiritual maturity through a process of inner reflection and development. Often, such people then end up being a decisive factor in changing their physical and social environments. So, either the environment alters the individual so that that person progresses; or the individual sets out to progress, ultimately altering his environment.

This means that anyone can eventually become an independent problem-solver, given the right environment in which to operate or the necessary inner motivation. Either way, the growing number of these societal members and their increasing impact on their environments means that a social revolution is eminent.

The Competition for Creativity

On an international scope, the competition between countries for these creative problem-solving workers is heating up. "For several years now, my colleagues and I have been measuring the underlying factors common to those American cities and regions with the highest level of creative economic growth. The chief factors we've found are: large numbers of talented individuals, a high degree of technological innovation, and a tolerance of diverse lifestyles. Recently my colleague Irene Tinagli of Carnegie Mellon and I have applied the same analysis to northern Europe, and the findings are startling. The playing field is much more level than you might think. Sweden tops the United States on this measure, with Finland, the Netherlands, and Denmark close behind. The United Kingdom and Belgium are also doing well. And most of these countries, especially Ireland, are becoming more creatively competitive at a faster rate than the United States."[46]

Additionally, members of this international independent problem-solving workforce, Creative Class, or Global Citizens, are becoming increasingly vocal about their disapproval of government incompetence and are underscoring their criticism by leaving the countries which refuse to change their policies. What follows is an account of an expatriate Australian currently living in Great Britain:

---

[46] Florida, Richard, "Creative Class War", Washington Monthly, January 15, 2004, Online: www.alternet.org

"This year 1 million Australians out of a population of 20 million are living outside Australia. Many Europeans who have given the best years of their lives to Australia have decided to cut their losses and return to the other side of the world. Go to Greece and you'll be astonished at how many Greeks speak fluent, idiomatic Australian. So why do so many abandon the 'you beaut' country? What can be the problem? I can best explain from my own point of view, as someone who left Australia in 1964, never to return...

Make no mistake. I love Australia with a fierce passion that churns my guts and makes my eyes burn with tears of rage and frustration. But I would rather not be there. For the vast majority, life in Australia is neither urban nor rural but suburban. The reality is not Uluru or the Sydney Opera House but endless, ever-expanding replications of Ramsay Street that spread out as rapidly as oil stains on water, further and further from the tiny central business districts of the state capitals...

The Australian economy is growing, we are told, faster than almost any other. Growth understood as a percentage is related to the initial size of the economy and Australia's remains tiny, even though it is the world's largest exporter of coal, iron ore, beef and wool. Coal and iron ore are obtained by massively mechanised open-cut mining, with devastating environmental consequences. The

Australian rush to self-destruction is a bewildering phenomenon.

Why does Australia destroy a greater percentage of its forests each year than all but two other countries on earth? In a mere 200 years one of the most bio-diverse systems in the world has been utterly compromised, and for what? Nobody is costing the degradation of fragile ecosystems by grazing or by irrigation for rice and cotton, crops that could never earn their keep unless the Australian dollar remained artificially low...

The real reason I won't live in Australia, even when Britain has no further use for my services, is that I love the country too much. The pain of watching its relentless dilapidation by people too relaxed to give a damn is more than I can bear. I don't know how many of my fellow expatriates feel this way, but I'll bet some do."[47]

This account includes many of the arguments of place listed previously in this chapter. Furthermore, the argumentation against the wanton destruction of the environment is a clear example of a postmodern value. This is also a value carried by the Creative Class, Global Citizens and a value touted by Independent Problem Solvers.

The recognition of changes created by the new job market has also caused a definite change in the way in which regional development and city renewal

---

[47] Anonymous, Slack and Insufferable, The Australian, Australia's National Daily Newspaper, Jan. 22, 2004

takes place. Although this trend is obvious in the United States, this same trend can be observed in many countries on the European continent, although the process is in its beginning stages there. "If governments want substantial numbers of well-paid citizens so that they can tax them, then it will be up to governments to provide the right conditions to create a climate conducive to well-paid citizens being willing to be taxed. Of course no one is yet suggesting that national governments won't be able to fix their levels of tax for the foreseeable future, but their increasingly nomadic citizens will be able to vote with their feet on whether they'll stay around to pay them."[48]

Currently, governments tend to try to entice large multinational companies to locate in an area in order to improve the fiscal condition of that community. Unfortunately, this method tends to create a situation where governments allow themselves to be held for ransom or they offer themselves to the highest (actually lowest) bidder. In reality, most current government policies call for offers of big tax incentives to entice companies to relocate.

At the first sign of possible interest from a corporation these communities compete heavily against other locations offering investment packages sometimes equaling a third of the total investment projected by the company. However, this kind of baiting does not insure that the companies will stay in that location for any given length of time. "For instance, in 1996 the Prime Minister of the Republic of Ireland,

---

[48] Makimoto, Tsugio; Manners, David; Digital Nomad,
    pg. 207

John Bruton, publicly complained about the nomadic propensities of some foreign companies. 'One Japanese company is worth three of any other kind...once here they don't leave.'"[49]

Also, as mentioned earlier, companies aren't being enticed by large tax incentives or infrastructural facilities anymore. Increasingly, many are foregoing any type of community support whatsoever for their location in order to settle in areas where they have the greatest amount of creative talent. Locating in an area in which there is a high density of creativity allows a company to pick and choose their workers and, through this, ensure their future economic and innovative growth.

So the tried-and-true method of economic development which has been slavishly followed by governments for the past 20 years has lost its credibility. Faced with the rising mobility of its citzenry as well as the extreme mobility of its most desirable citizens, communities and governments will now have to compete aggressively for *citizens*. This is necessary because of the fact that cities and governments receive their operating revenue through tax income. If they lose citizens or the highly paid independent problem-solving citizens, they lose taxes. The loss of taxes in turn causes a reduction in the quality of services offered and subsequently causes that area to become more unattractive.

---

[49] Makimoto, Tsugio; Manners, David; Digital Nomad, pg. 209

Ultimately, this development further encourages the citizens, or more appropriately the necessary independent problem-solving citizens living there to move to somewhere more "livable". But is the reverse scenario equally true? Will improving the quality of life within an area cause more creative people to want to live there?

There are a number of very interesting examples of cities where just exactly **that** happened and is currently happening. These cities decided that they would use the tax income and funding which they had in order to improve the quality of life in their city and not to chase after foreign investment. The result was that the city became so attractive that it drew people and companies to it. One of the most important examples of this phenomenon in recent years was and is Fort Collins, Colorado, USA. This city will be closely examined later in this chapter.

The growth in the number of and in the increase in the financial clout of the new independent problem solvers has fueled the growth of a new type of development. This new development type carries many names. Among these names are: New Urbanism, Smart Growth, Sustainable Development, Anti-Sprawl Development, Community Density and Sensible Growth. The following chapter section will explore this phenomenon and site notable examples of this new type of development.

2.2 Sensible Growth, Anti-Sprawl, New-Urbanism, and Natural Capitalism / Sustainability

"If we wish to make a new world, we have the material ready. The first one, too, was made out of chaos."
Robert Quillen

The emergence of a new and economically potent class of people, the new independent problem-solving work elite or the Creative Class, has caused remarkable changes in all facets of society. Among these changes is the growing awareness of problems beyond the person survival level. As observed by Ronald Inglehart and initially by Abraham Maslow, through the reduction in the necessity to constantly provide for survival, human beings are freed to concentrate on higher goals and purposes.

This phenomenon could clearly be observed within the United States in the time period before the worldwide economic crisis of 2008-2009, where the reduction in time necessary to provide for survival allowed citizens to actively join in the development and re-development of their communities. This increased community activism was given many different names; however, the purpose of these groups was remarkably similar: to alter and improve the livability of communities through the reduction in wasted land and energy and to promote an increase in amenities which improve standard of living.

Sensible Growth / Smart Growth / Anti-Sprawl
Sparked by the increasing importance and awareness of community development issues, the United States Environmental Protection Agency created the National Award for Smart Growth Achievement in 2002. This award was developed to highlight the achievements of communities throughout the United States with regard to the reduction of wasteland, the reduction of pollution caused by increased driving distances, and the promotion of density in a community (a feature which is critical to the support of the other goals).

The U.S. Environmental Protection Agency noted the nationwide trend in focus on Smart Growth issues by citing the following statistics: "Between 2001 and 2002, the number of smart growth developments increased by 26%; More than 6,000 main street and downtown revitalization projects are underway throughout the country (2003); and 75% of all parks and open space ballot measures on local and state ballots in 2002 were passed by voters—an increase from 70% in 2001."[50] When one examines the cited statistics carefully, an increased public interest in these types of issues becomes apparent.

But the United States government is not the only institution within the United States which is dealing with this developing trend. The Campaign for Sensible Growth is a non-government organization based in the Midwestern United States whose

---

[50] United States Environmental Protection Agency, National Award for Smart Growth Achievement, 2003 (pamphlet), Office of Policy, Economics and Innovation (1808-T), EPA 231-F-03-002, November 2003

purpose is to link all communities and interested parties on the issue of sensible community growth. A regular newsletter distributed by the organization through e-mail provides members with up-to-date information on sensible growth issues, articles, trends and events. The organization supports the trend that it is informing about, by providing a timely forum for its members.[51] Although Campaign for Sensible Growth's membership consists primarily of organizations and interested parties in the Midwestern United States, similar organizations can be found throughout the United States.

An increasing dominance of environmental protection issues is a reflection of a worldwide change in values documented through the World Values Survey. Within the built environment this growth in emphasis on these types of issues has caused built community forms to undergo a drastic change. No longer is the practice of building upon green areas (farmland) as economically feasible as it once was. This is due to the fact that many U.S. communities are buying up farmland immediately surrounding them in an effort to stem unhindered sprawl. By purchasing farmland around their communities they are taking a proactive step against outside commercial interests, like land developers.

Additionally, other communities are passing stricter zoning laws which restrict development of these farmlands. This change in policy is a direct result of an increased awareness of the long-term costs of allowing unchecked farmland development.

---

[51] http://www."Campaign for Sensible Growth" <listserv@growingsensibly.org

Many communities in the United States have conducted surveys in addition to financing studies on the long-term costs and detriments of urban sprawl. In almost all of the studies, the resulting cost calculation caused a change in the attitude of the community towards urban sprawl and provided a basis for legislative prohibition of farmland development. "A report by the U.S. Office of Technology Assessment (OTA) found that it cost a western city $10,000 more to provide infrastructure to a lower density suburban development than to a more compact urban neighborhood. Similarly, the Urban Land Institute (ULI) found that infrastructure costs per housing unit drop dramatically as density increases. The combined cost of Utilities, schools, and streets falls from $90,000 for one dwelling sited on four acres to just over $10,000 per unit for developments of 30 units per acre. (OTA-ETI-643, 1995; ULI, Wieman, 1996)."[52]

By prohibiting unchecked growth into the surrounding farmlands, communities in the United States have created an environment in which the redevelopment of inner-city wasteland has once again become economically viable. With the emphasis of new buildings and real estate projects being placed within the built-up city limits, density has once again become a key issue. The collapse of the real estate bubble in the US and the overabundance of large suburban tracts of enormous vacant houses,

---

[52] Local Government Commission; United States Environmental Protection Agency, Creating Great Neighborhoods: Density in Your Community (pamphlet), National Association of Realtors, September 2003, pg. 7

known as McMansions, has caused a shift in values and a buyer's market. Coupled with the growing energy prices, many potential homeowners are chosing to locate in denser communities, where a second family car is no longer a financial necessity. The choice for a smaller, more affordable home in a denser urban environment brings with it an increase in overall quality-of-life. As a result, density, an aspect of the best urban environments and an attribute cited unceasingly by Jane Jacobs (The Death and Life of Great American Cities), has regained its position within the urban renewal community as well as within community governments themselves.

Increased density of the built environment also supports the protection of the environment, a value of the independent problem solvers "Higher-density development expands transportation choices by making it easier to use non-automobile transportation–walking, bicycling, (and) bus and rail transit– by locating activities closer together. Studies indicate that the average resident in a compact neighborhood will drive 20 to 30 percent less than residents of a neighborhood half as dense."[53]

Additionally: "At densities of eight units per acre and higher, neighborhoods begin to support bus and rail transit by increasing the number of transit users within walking and bicycling distance of a bus or rail station. Some areas refer to eight housing units per acre to support minimal bus service (30-minute

---

[53] Local Government Commission; United States Environmental Protection Agency, Creating Great Neighborhoods: Density in Your Community (pamphlet), National Association of Realtors, September 2003, pg. 6

headways), 20 units per acre to support a transit station, or 30 units per acre to support high-frequency transit service (10-minute headways)."[54] The economic viability of public transportation increases as the density of the built environment increases.

Along with density, the United States Environmental Protection Agency encourages additional smart growth principles. "The principles of smart growth include:

1. Mix land uses.
2. Take advantage of compact building design.
3. Create housing opportunities and choices for a range of household types, family sizes and incomes.
4. Create walkable neighborhoods.
5. Foster distinctive, attractive communities with a strong sense of place.
6. Preserve open space, farmland, natural beauty and critical environmental areas.
7. Reinvest in and strengthen existing communities and achieve more balanced regional development.
8. Provide a variety of transportation choices.
9. Make development decisions predictable, fair and cost-effective.

---

[54] Local Government Commission; United States Environmental Protection Agency, Creating Great Neighborhoods: Density in Your Community (pamphlet), National Association of Realtors, September 2003, pg. 6, see also Holtzclaw, John, www.sierraclub.org/sprawl/articles/designing.asp

10. Encourage citizen and stakeholder
participation in development decisions."[55]

Interestingly enough, a comparison and analysis of
the community traits espoused by the United States
Environmental Protection Agency bears a striking
resemblance to the qualities of place sought by the
Creative Class. A similarity with these characteristics
can be determined by revisiting the list of these traits
found on page 44-46 of this work.

Bearing this in mind, it quickly becomes evident
that the values of this group of individuals must be
becoming so influential, that they are even reaching
the higher levels of government. This means that it is
only a matter of time before the major power positions within governments are held by these people.

The economic and societal dominance of this class
of people has influenced and is continuing to
influence the course of community development. The
previous emphasis on unchecked urban sprawl and
farmland subdivisions is being replaced by an
increasing emphasis on smart growth and smart
growth principles. This, in turn, has resulted in the
re-creation of a new/old form of urban development
dubbed New Urbanism.

---

[55] United States Environmental Protection Agency, National
Award for Smart Growth Achievement, 2003 (pamphlet),
Office of Policy, Economics and Innovation (1808-T), EPA
231-F-03-002, November 2003

New Urbanism

New Urbanism is a widely spread trend in alternative development which had its origin in the USA. This movement originated from the concerns of building professionals with relation to the environmental impact of continued suburban sprawl development. As noted earlier, concerns for the environment are a postmodern value and are prevalent in most countries of the world in differing degrees.

The first Congress of New Urbanism, held in 1993, was a meeting of about 170 designers organized to compare works-in-progress and exchange ideas about urban and suburban places. Architects Peter Calthorpe, Andres Duany, Elizabeth Moule, Stefanos Polyzoides, Elizabeth Plater-Zyberk, and Daniel Solomon, along with organizer Peter Katz, developed the CNU as a non-profit organization to promote and disseminate information about New Urbanism. The CNU Charter was developed between 1993 and 1996. It was eventually ratified during the fourth annual congress in Charleston, South Carolina. This trend can be viewed as a backlash reaction of homeowners and designers to the prevalent form of community development.

Tired of an automobile oriented and impersonal lifestyle offered by these traditional subdivisions, the New Urbanism homeowner seeks a community type reminiscent of the inner-city neighborhoods of the late 19th and early 20th centuries. New Urbanism neighborhoods include sidewalks; a mixed-use development; town squares—where the main community functions are located; and a compact community development which allows community members to run errands by walking or riding their bikes. A major additional feature of these communities is their tendency to include large areas of undeveloped space—a close proximity to nature. As noted in the previous chapter section, these qualities are features sought by the growing creative portion of society.

Additionally, as the creative societal members are those with the larger pocketbooks, the National Real Estate Board of the United States has noted that homes in New Urbanism developments tend to achieve higher resale prices than homes in traditional American suburban communities. These statements were based upon a study completed by the National Center for Smart Growth Research and Education at the University of Maryland which compared the resale prices of 48,000 single-family homes in the Portland, Oregon area. The study found that "homes in intimate and highly planned neighborhoods fetch(ed) 15.5% more than comparable homes in traditional subdivisions."[56]

Whereas, according to the study, home buyers are willing to "pay a premium for elements like connected street networks, smaller blocks, better pedestrian access to shops and proximity to light rail"; the study also concluded that these same home buyers who "are willing to pay a premium to be near these elements,...don't actually want to live in the thick of them."[57] The inconsistency rests with the different needs of the various home buyers. Single-family homeowners purchase a home in order to

[56] Frangos, Alex: "What's New Urbanism Worth?", Wall Street Journal (Eastern edition), December 24, 2003, pg. B6.
[57] ibid.

achieve a certain degree of privacy. Purchasers of apartments, on the other hand, seek to be in the middle of activities.

This explains the discrepancy within the study. "John K. McIlwain, a senior resident fellow at the Urban Land Institute in Washington, D.C., isn't surprised that people pay more for homes in new urbanist areas, but questions the notion that density is a negative in pricing. The study "splits things apart that have to be looked at together," he says. "If you are going to use land intensively, how you design it and the amenities you include are critical.""[58]

New Urbanism has also been, possibly more correctly, called "neo-traditionalism". An internet real estate sales ad explains:

"Dubbed "neo-traditionalism," this new approach features classically-styled houses of various shapes, sizes and values, clustered along friendly, tree-lined streets and attractive public parks or playgrounds. Neighborhoods are laid out in grids rather than cul-de-sacs, and cars are tucked behind houses, not garaged or parked in front. Homes have front porches and, thanks to generous shared spaces, smaller lots than normal. Sidewalks encourage walking to and from local businesses and, with the help of public transportation, reduce reliance upon cars."[59]

[58] Frangos, Alex: "What's New Urbanism Worth?", Wall Street Journal (Eastern edition), December 24, 2003, pg. B6
[59] http://www.hometips.com

Some of the most notable of these new communities are: Seaside, Florida; Kentlands, outside Washington, D.C.; Harbor Town, near Memphis, Tennessee; Laguna West, near Sacramento, California; and possibly the most famous of the group Celebration, Florida, a community planned and developed by the Walt Disney Corporation. All of these communities were designed based on the principles of new urbanism mentioned above. By using the new urbanism principles, designers created places which offered residents increased levels of quality of life not available in traditional residential developments.

Although initially developed as a "new" innovational return to the best design practices of previous centuries, New Urbanism is a planning idea which will continue to grow in strength over the next decades. Supported by a rise in the price of gasoline, communities of this type, where the homeowner only needs one or no automobile at all, will grow in popularity. It is quite possible that the planning ideals of New Urbanism will be integrated with green technologies in the future to create an entirely new developmental strategy in which building requirements and the needs of the environment are fused together.

Parallel to the expansion of the ideals of New Urbanism, another idea has been steadily gaining momentum. Sustainability is another product of the advancement of the values of the independent problem solvers and its development is worth examining closely as a means of gaining a greater understanding of their character and their values.

Sustainability – Agenda 21 / Urban 21

In 1972, the United Nations organized an international conference which was held in Stockholm, Sweden. The conference was called the UN Conference on the Human Environment and had as its focus, the state of the global environment. It was the first conference of its type in the world. Governments set up the United Nations Environment Programme (sic) (UNEP), following the conference. This program "continues to act as a global catalyst for action to protect the environment."[60] However, little was done in the following years by the nations to integrate environmental concerns into their national economic planning and their general decision-making. Despite the lack of implementation, this conference provided the framework for the beginning of a new way of looking at worldwide development.

In 1983, the United Nations set up the World Commission on Environment and Development. This commission found that the environmental degradation "which had been seen as a side effect of industrial wealth with only a limited impact, was understood to be a matter of survival for developing nations."[61] As a result, the commission produced a concept of sustainable development "as an alternative approach to one simply based on economic growth–one 'which meets the needs of the present without compromising the ability of future generations to meet their own needs'."[62]

[60] http://www.un.org/geninfo/bp/envirp2.html
[61] ibid.
[62] ibid.

This paper, officially known as the Brundtland Report (after Gro Harlem Brundtland of Norway), caused a stir in the United Nations General Assembly. After considering this report, the General Assembly called for a conference on the environment and development. "The primary goals of the Summit were to come to an understanding of 'development' that would support socio-economic development and prevent the continued deterioration of the environment, and to lay a foundation for a global partnership between the developing and the more industrialized countries, based on mutual needs and common interests, that would ensure a healthy future for the planet."[63]

In December of 1989, a process of planning, education and negotiations was started among all Member States of the United Nations which culminated in the two-week Earth Summit in Rio de Janeiro in 1992. The ensuing conference officially titled "The United Nations Conference on Environment and Development (UNCED), unofficially titled "The Earth Summit", held in Rio de Janeiro, Brazil attracted quite a number of participants. The number of governments participating in the conference was 172, of those, 108 participants were at the level of heads of state or government.

The principal theme of this conference was the environment and sustainable development. The resulting documents produced were three agreements: Agenda 21; The Rio Declaration on Environment and Development; the Statement of Forest Principles; and two legally binding Conventions: the United Nations

---

[63] http://www.un.org/geninfo/bp/envirp2.html

Framework Convention on Climate Change; and the United Nations Convention on Biological Diversity. These documents created a framework upon which the participating nations agreed to base the future development of their countries.

"The Earth Summit in Rio de Janeiro was unprecedented for a UN conference, in terms of both its size and the scope of its concerns. Twenty years after the first global environment conference, the UN sought to help Governments rethink economic development and find ways to halt the destruction of irreplaceable natural resources and pollution of the planet."[64]

The message of the summit was that nothing less than a transformation of the current attitudes and behaviors would bring about any substantial changes in the condition of the planet. Among other important points, the "governments recognized the need to redirect international and national plans and policies to ensure that all economic decisions fully took into account any environmental impact."[65]

Whereas Agenda 21 represented a program of comprehensive action for global activities in all areas of sustainable development; the Rio Declaration on Environment and Development provided a series of principles defining the rights and responsibilities of the states with regard to the environment and development. The third major agreement adopted at the Earth Summit was the Statement of Forest Principles which was a set of principles to underlie the sustainable management of forests worldwide.

---

[64] http:///www.un.org/geninfo/bp/enviro.html
[65] ibid.

Two legally binding conventions were also opened for signature at the summit. The conventions were focused on trying to prevent global climate change and the subsequent eradication of the diversity of biological species.

All of these documents emphasized the pressing need felt by many nations to regulate the exploitation of the planet and to encourage the development of alternative forms of energy and alternative methods of development. Of these five documents, Agenda 21 presented the most comprehensive scheme of future developmental goals in all aspects of society encompassing both the physical aspects and the social aspects of societal development. The Rio Declaration on Environment and Development was the accompanying document to Agenda 21 and defined the rights and responsibilities of the member states on the included issues.

The Earth Summit and its resulting documentation constituted the first global attempt at creating a catalog of criteria for future physical, economic, social, and environmental development and for measuring the global effectiveness of such development. The most important of the documents produced as a result of the Earth Summit in 1992 was an agreement called Agenda 21. This agreement was aimed, among the other agreements signed during that two week conference, at changing the traditional approach to development and created a concept called sustainability.

In an effort to encourage compliance with the statutes included in the Agenda agreement, the Earth Summit called on the General Assembly of the United Nations to establish a commission with those functions. Thus the UN Commission on Sustainable Development (CSD) was created.

Agenda 21 has a number of sectoral issues—these are; health, human settlements, freshwater, toxic chemicals and hazardous waste, land, agriculture, desertification, mountains, forests, biodiversity, atmosphere, and oceans and seas. Between 1994 and 1996 the UN Commission of Sustainable Development monitored the early implementation of Agenda 21. The issues were clustered to create more effective areas for monitoring. The resulting clusters are: "critical elements of sustainability which are the areas of trade and environment, patterns of production and consumption, combating poverty, and democratic dynamics; financial resources and mechanisms; education, science, the transfer of environmentally sound technologies, and technical cooperation and capacity-building; decision-making, and activities of the major groups, such as business and labor."[66]

"Central to the ability of Governments to formulate policies for sustainability and to regulate their impact is the development of a set of internationally accepted criteria and indicators for sustainable development."[67] So the Commission on Sustainable Development set out to develop these criteria. Eventually, a menu of indicators will be produced which will enable countries to use them to cultivate their national plans and strategies. These general indicators will also ease the work of the Commission in monitoring each country's progress.

---

[66] http://www.un.org/geninfo/bp/envirp3.html
[67] ibid.

In 2002 the world met again, this time, however, in Johannesburg, South Africa. The goal of this second "Earth Summit" was to monitor the progress on the implementation of the goals set forth during the Earth Summit in 1992. Questions such as: "What has been accomplished since 1992, have participating countries ratified the conventions that aim to prevent loss of biodiversity or ensure women's rights as they agreed to in 1992?"[68], etc. were covered within the course of the United Nations Summit. Unfortunately, the information gathered at the second "Earth Summit" indicated that the implementation of the sustainability criteria was progressing at a very slow pace, if at all. In December of 2005 the trend of shorter time periods between major world summits on environmental issues continued with the World Climate Conference in Montreal, Canada followed a few years later by the conference in Copenhagen and the latest in December of 2010 in Mexico.

In 2000, as part of the EXPO 2000 in Hanover, Germany, the German Federal Ministry of Construction and Urbanism organized a three day "World Conference on the Future of Cities" in Berlin. Within the framework of the criteria in Agenda 21, this conference, taking place from July 4th through July 6th, 2000, examined the future of the city and subsequently produced a list of sustainability criteria specifically directed at cities. The sustainability of cities was discussed and the criteria produced executed the directive given through the Earth Summit in 1992.

---

[68] http://www.earthcharter.org/wssd/

Organized by the Federal Ministry of Construction and Urbanism and hosted by the Federal Republic of Germany, as well as the governments of Brazil, Singapore and South Africa, this conference was attended by a number of experts in the field of city planning and development from around the world. Notable among these was: Dr. Ela Bhatt, from the Self-employed Women's Association in Ahmedabad, India; Professor Sir Peter Hall, from London; Mark Malloch Brown, the Administrator of the United Nations Development Programme (UNDP) in New York; as well as notables from Brazil, Germany, Singapore, Russia, Nairobi–Kenya, and China.

An emphasis was placed on quality of life issues during the conference. It was discovered that quality of life criteria had changed very little throughout the centuries. "In the 21st Century, the quality of life for a majority of humankind will be the quality of the life they lead in cities. They (the inhabitants of these cities) will surely want what people have wanted throughout history: satisfying work that yields sufficiency of income and freedom from poverty; living in well-integrated societies with stable social networks,...existing in a state of ecological harmony and balance with the wider natural environment; having adequate mobility to reach work, shops, children's schools, friends and recreational opportunities; acting as citizens within a political system that offers balanced representation of interests and values; served with adequate public services from sewers to schools, respecting the basic needs of all people living in the city; and dwelling in a built environment that preserves tradition but serves the needs of modern economic life and modern lifestyles."[69]

The commission also acknowledged that while these quality of life issues are part of common knowledge, they are very difficult to apply globally and equally throughout cities. Although the commission accepted the fact that economic and social differences exist within the world, it also expressed optimism that the coming technology will allow a number of existing problems to be solved. One of the main points discussed during the conference was the difference in problems facing the cities in the industrialized world, and those facing cities in the developing world.

The major problem facing the industrialized nations is the declining city populations and the reduction in the birth rate of the populations. In some European cities the birth rate has dipped as low as 13 or 14 per thousand. This is a dangerous trend and leads to a tremendous imbalance between the young (who pay taxes) and the old (who receive these taxes in the form of social security). Seeing the danger of having to pay exorbitant taxes to support an aging population and, with the coming possibilities offered through the new technologies (Digital Nomadism), these young people might seek to escape the burdens of the tax structure for countries and cities where this is not the case.

The commission itself offered proposals as to how to improve the situation in these cities and countries for the inhabitants. These included: a refor-

---

[69] World Commission Urban 21, World Report on the Urban Future – URBAN 21, pp. 12-13

mation of taxation and pension systems in order to reduce the burden of taxes; a deregulation of markets in order to intensify competition; a reformation of the public sector to increase efficiency; a reduction of collectively funded pension entitlements in order to encourage private savings; and a creation of funded pensions in order to increase lifetime savings and lifetime work through later retirement. Implementing suggestions such as these would lead to a stronger middle class and a stronger younger class and would be an incentive for stability of residency.

Sustainability, therefore, is a planning and development concept designed to view man-made, industrial, as well as environmental entities as part of a closed ecosystem. This means that sustainability acknowledges that any changes to an entity will cause changes to the rest of the ecosystem. In order to develop long-term solutions to existing problems it is therefore necessary to examine a possible solution to a problem within the context of possible ramifications caused by implementing the offered solution.

A sustainable solution to a problem is thus one which benefits all segments of society and the ecosystem while it solves the problem. This holistic approach to problem-solving is a new concept within modern societies and reflects a global change in value systems documented in Inglehart's <u>Modernization and Postmodernization</u>. It is also a value very intrinsic to the core ideals of the independent problem solvers.

Sustainability–Factor 10, Factor 4 and Natural Capitalism

Parallel to governmental recognition for the need for sustainable development, a quiet revolution was also taking place in the industrial sector of society. A movement toward radical resource productivity was under way which reached a high-point in the fall of 1994. A conference was called by Friedrich Schmidt-Bleek of the Wuppertal Institute for Climate, Environment, and Energy in Germany and a group of sixteen scientists, economists, government officials, and businesspeople from all parts of the world including; Europe, the United States, Japan, England, Canada, and India participated in this conference. As a result of this conference, which was held in the French village of Carnoules, the "Carnoules Declaration" was published.

The conclusion of the members of the conference was that they believed that "human activities were at risk from the ecological and social impact of materials and energy use".[70] The group called for a radical increase in resource productivity in order to stem or reverse the growing damage. Later calling itself the Factor 10 Club, the group began its published declaration by stating that: "Within one generation, nations can achieve a ten-fold increase in the efficiency with which they use energy, natural resources and other materials."[71] Following this conference and resulting from the attention that the declaration

---

[70] Hawken, Paul; Lovins, Amory; Lovins, L. Hunter; Natural Capitalism, pg. 11

[71] Schmidt-Bleek et al, „Statement to Government and Business Leaders", Wuppertal Institute, 1997

received, Factor 10 (a 90 percent reduction in energy and materials intensity) and Factor Four (a 75 percent reduction) began to be accepted by various government officials, planners, academics and businesspeople throughout the world.

By September 1996, the Factor 10 Club had grown to include participants from: UNEPIE, Paris; the Institut für Produktdauerforschung, Giebenach, Switzerland; the Institute for Environment and Systems Analysis, Amsterdam; the Business Council for Sustainable Development; Dow Europe; the Institute of Ecotoxicology, Gakushuin University, Tokyo; the Dutch Sustainable Technology Programme; Development Alternatives, New Delhi; the Institute for Labor and Technology, Gelsenkirchen, Germany; the Brundtland Commission, Ottawa, Canada; Greenpeace Germany; Osaka University; the Wuppertal Institute, Wuppertal, Germany; the Institute de la Durabilité, Geneva, Switzerland; the Center for Eco-Efficiency and Enterprise, University of Portsmouth, the World Business Council for Sustainable Development, Geneva; the Austrian Association for Agro-scientific Research; and the Institute of Industry Science at the University of Tokyo.[72]

Subsequently, "the governments of Austria, the Netherlands, and Norway have publicly committed to pursuing Factor Four efficiencies. The same approach has been endorsed by the European Union as the new paradigm for sustainable development. Austria, Sweden, and OECK environment ministers have urged the adoption of Factor Ten goals, as have the World Business Council for Sustainable Develop-

---

[72] Hawken et. al., Natural Capitalism, pg. 323

ment and the United Nations Environment Program (UNEP).[73]/[74] But governments aren't the only institutions that have come to realize that a radical improvement in the use of resources is necessary for the sustainable development of the world; industries are also starting to take notice. Companies such as Dow Europe and Mitsubishi Electric have realized that an implementation of the Factor 10 principles can possibly lead to an economic advantage over their competitors.

This is and was the genius of these principles: that an increase in the efficient use of raw materials can not only improve environmental factors by reducing waste, it can also increase productivity and profits. This means that companies no longer need to resist the ecological point of view as being detrimental to business; they can embrace it and by embracing it, improve their profit margins and their company's productivity. This is an entirely new concept in ecological circles and means that the two sides of the ecological coin no longer had to be diametrically opposed.

Beyond an increase in resource productivity which includes "obtaining the same amount of utility or work from a product or process while using less material and energy"[75], there is increasing evidence that radical resource productivity is being pursued by a group of companies and designers that seek to increase the resource productivity by five, ten or

[73] Hawken et. al., Natural Capitalism, pg. 12
[74] Gardner, G.; Sampat, P., „Mind over Matter: Recasting the Role of Materials in Our Lives", 1998
[75] Hawken, et. al., Natural Capitalism, pg. 12

even one hundred times the current levels. This radical increase would not only reduce the cost of production through saved resources but could potentially reduce initial capital investments in production and ultimately improve the quality of life through reductions in noise, air and water pollution.

So the trend in growing resource productivity is essentially a mass appeal for radical efficiency in all aspects of our lives. This new-found efficiency should also include the efficient use of human resources as well. Since it is generally known that almost all governments in the world operate at an abysmal level of efficiency, this is a major potential area for improvement. Parallel to that, an increase in efficiency within the industrial sector of society will bring equally impressive results. At this point, a small community in Bavaria, Germany is certainly worth mentioning.

In May of 1996, Jürgen Spahl, the former head of the Building Department of Rednitzhembach, Germany was elected mayor of the community. His new job would not be an easy one, as the community had debts approaching 5 million Euros. Calculated based upon the population, this was a per capita debt of approximately 780 Euros. In addition to the problem of the mounting debt, the personnel costs in the community were increasing and the community council had just passed bills approving new building projects which would cost additional millions.

In order to combat the problem, Jürgen Spahl began by convincing his constituents that something radical needed to be done. He started the reformation process by describing the problems in terms that everyone could understand. He explained that the community was paying 1300 Euros in interest each and every day, the equivalent to some of the citizen's monthly salaries. He then started on a course of radical simplification of the governmental structure within the community. By convincing employees to give up their full-time positions for part-time positions, and by offering them more autonomy, he was able to radically cut personnel costs.[76]

Although critics claimed the idea would never work, the acceptance of the new scheme was very high. As noted previously, Postmodern employees are more interested in obtaining a level of personal satisfaction from work than in receiving a great deal of money. This transfer of authority had the additional effect of increasing the efficiency of the bureaucratic apparatus, cutting the time needed to receive necessary building permits and certificates dramatically. In one case a company was so impressed with this new efficiency that they made a decision to relocate to Rednitzhembach and purchased the necessary property only two hours after meeting with city officials for the first time.[77]

This newfound efficiency also encouraged families in the surrounding communities to relocate to Rednitzhembach. Consequently, the population increased by seven percent during the mayor's first term of office. The presence of adequate amounts of Kindergarten facilities and a good school system also led to an influx of inhabitants. This is a concrete

---

[76] Sachse, Katrin, „Null-Euro-Miese-Dorf", Focus 46/2003, pg. 54
[77] ibid.

example of applying the principals expounded upon in this book. By providing the social infrastructure needed, as defined by the level of needs currently required, a community can create a social magnet attracting highly-paid independent problem-solvers which will, in turn, lead to an increased tax base.

But perhaps the most impressive results of all resulted from the community's complete departure from the normal method of building. Here the mayor abandoned the traditional community building system of obtaining multiple bids in order to receive government building subsidies in favor of creating a private/public firm to manage all community building projects. According to the calculations of the mayor, this method of building saved approximately 20% of the cost of construction per project. This represents a radical savings over the traditional method of building within communities.

The result of all of these reforms was that the community reduced its debt from a whopping 4,877,920 Euros to 0 Euros within 7 years time while, at the same time, investing millions in the infrastructure of their community.[78] This is a 100% increase in efficiency and exactly within the framework of goals set by Factor 10. If the results achieved in the community of Rednitzhembach are any indication of the potential inherent in applying the rules of Factors 10 and 4 and the principles of Natural Capitalism (see Figure 4)[79], then commun-

[78] Sachse, Katrin, „Null-Euro-Miese-Dorf", Focus 46/2003, pg. 54-57
[79] Hawken, et. al., Natural Capitalism, pg. 10-11

ities and businesses worldwide would do well to the employ them.

The world conferences which produced Agenda 21 and Urban 21 and the increasing movement within the business environment toward Natural Capitalism sets the stage for a decided shift in the focus of the World's development strategy and indicates an alteration in the way human beings throughout the world view economic success. The success of the few

---

Principles of Natural Capitalism

1. **Radical Resource Productivity**—a radical increase in resource productivity has three benefits: It slows resource depletion, lowers pollution and provides the basis to increase worldwide employment in meaningful jobs.

2. **Biomimicry**—requires changing the nature of industrial processes/materials in order to reduce the wasteful throughput of materials by designing continuous closed cycles which result in the elimination of toxicity.

3. **Service and Flow Economy**—calls for a shift in the relationship between producer and consumer, changing the economy from one of goods and purchases to one of service and flow. This includes a change in attitude from one in which the possession of goods has the highest priority to one in which the receipt of quality, utility and performance promotes well-being.

4. **Investing in Natural Capital**—reversing the worldwide planetary destruction by investing in sustaining, restoring and expanding stocks of natural capital.

Figure 4. Principles of Natural Capitalism
Source: Author

---

at the expense of the many has been the dominating business philosophy over the last few decades.

The rampant destruction of the environment and severe economic crises have also resulted from this business methodology, but international organizations representing the ideals and values of the drivers of the coming social revolution are countering. Documents leaked to watchdog organizations like Wikileaks and Transparency International are leading the way in exposing excessive corporate greed and dangerous business practices. In light of natural disasters caused by profit driven greed and incompetence (such as the Deepwater Horizon oil rig catastrophy) this is a welcome advance.

These changes are also indicative of the advancement of the number of independent problem solvers throughout the world. Once again, the effect is reciprocal. Either a society is set up in such a way that it provides all of the necessary conditions in order to facilitate the advancement of a person to the level of an independent problem solver or healthy human being; or the number of healthy human beings in a society reaches a critical mass and these people then begin to advance their ideals and values within a society.

Sensible Growth, New Urbanism, Sustainability and Natural Capitalism are all ideas generated by independent problem solvers or healthy human beings. The growth and expansion of these values is indicative of the increase in the number of these societal members and the advancement of their scope of influence. The next chapter section will examine best-practice examples of sustainable city development throughout the world.

2.3 Re-Urbanization, New Urbanism and Natural Capitalism/Sustainability Examples

"What's remarkable about Fort Collins is not all it has done to lure companies (to locate to Fort Collins); it's all it hasn't done."[80]

City Re-Urbanization Examples

Somewhere along the line, decision makers within cities came up with the idea that luring international companies to move into their city would bring prosperity. Nothing could be further from the truth. As mentioned previously, the same companies that are willing to locate to a specific city are just as willing to relocate to a different city if the incentive package is large enough. This is reason enough to examine cities that succeeded in attracting the international companies without "selling their soul". On another level, highly innovative companies are increasingly ignoring the incentives offered by cities and are choosing to locate to areas which offer them the greatest choice in qualified workers. The truth is, only the cities which succeed in luring these highly creative and qualified workers will ultimately succeed in improving their economic condition.

Here is a case example: In 1995, Fort Collins, Colorado, USA, had the opportunity to get a major international company to move into its city. Hyndai Electronics Industries Co. (Hynix Semiconductor

---

[80] Gavin, Robert, "Getting a Lift – The Rockies Emerge as Pocket of Prosperity in a Slowing Economy", The Wall Street Journal, Wednesday, June 6, 2001.

Inc.) was willing to relocate to Fort Collins and build a 1.3 billion dollar semiconductor plant to employ 1,000 people. In exchange, the company wanted 30 million dollars in tax breaks which represented 10% of the city's annual budget.

The vote was close, 4:3 against the measure. Thereafter, the city decided to use its annual budget to invest in the community, building up the school system, increasing the amount of park area, improving the public transportation system, and restoring the downtown area. In 1996 the city adopted a master plan which has as its goal to add 7 acres of parkland for each additional 1000 citizens. The city council adopted the plan and provided the necessary development funding. Essentially, these were all things which improved the quality of life within the city for its citizens.

The improvements continued. Along with other entities, the city converted an old unused hotel into affordable housing for senior citizens. Located in the downtown area, this conversion provided affordable housing located close to all of the city's amenities (a principle of New Urbanism). In 2000, the city created a concrete park for its young citizens. This park was developed so that the youth could have a place to enjoy skateboarding, rollerblading and biking.

One of the most innovative of the improvement strategies occurred as a response to an increase in population and in subsequent traffic congestion. Businesses are now offered free use of bicycles which can be checked out by their employees in order to run errands, go to lunch and to go to meetings within the city. In 2001, 50 businesses and numerous city and county departments participated in the bicycle program, called "Free-wheels". This saved approximately "2,500 vehicle miles and more than 31,000 tons of carbon dioxide"[81], improving traffic congestion and air quality within the city.

Along with the improvement and augmentation of the public amenities within the city, Fort Collins concentrated on restoring their historic downtown. The historic downtown of Fort Collins served as a model for "Main Street U.S.A." in Disneyland. The charm or image of the city (Richard Florida termed it Authenticity and Identity), as well as other amenities, is a big factor in holding residents and companies in the city. "When San Diego based Applied Micro Circuits Corp. acquired Fort Collins telecommunications and data storage start-up Silutia Inc. last fall, Silutia executives made sure any talk of leaving Fort Collins was off the table. That 'would have been a deal-breaker,' says Randy Zwetzig, Silutia's former chief executive. 'We have beautiful summers, fairly mild winters, a strong education system, parks and safe neighborhoods.'"[82]

What has all of this improvement to the city and its public spaces achieved? The population of Fort Collins has nearly doubled in the last 25 years. Now a city of 118,000, Fort Collins offers a lot of amenities which a much larger city might not have: a school score which is among the best in the state of Colorado, theater, shopping, art fairs in addition to amenities which it has as a result of its location–

[81] City of Fort Collins, Colorado, City Scape: A Portrait of Progress-2001 Report to the Community, pg. 3

[82] Gavin, Robert, "Getting a Lift – The Rockies Emerge as Pocket of Prosperity in a Slowing Economy", The Wall Street Journal, Wednesday, June 6, 2001.

skiing, horseback riding, as well as hiking and other nature facilities.

Resulting from an increase in population, the tax base has increased and the city uses this increased tax base to perpetuate the cycle—once again investing the increased revenues into infrastructure and amenities. However, an increase in population was not the only result of this effort. Companies seeking to relocate and to attract qualified employees chose Fort Collins over other locations, even without receiving tax incentives. "During a time of economic slowdown across the country, the Rocky Mountain region is emerging as an island of surprising prosperity and growth. When companies and workers fled California during its deep recession of the early 1990s, Rocky Mountain communities offered low costs, an emerging technology sector and an alluring lifestyle. Since then, highly skilled and educated people have been flocking to emerging tech centers such as Boulder, Boise, and Provo, Utah, making Colorado, Idaho and Utah among the five fastest-growing states in the country."[83]

A large portion of the credit for the renewal of Fort Collins can be given to its citizens. Early in the renewal process the city began including citizens in all of its efforts. Part of this process was an annual Citizen Satisfaction Survey which proposed new efforts and rated the old ones. Through this integrated approach to city renewal they have found that citizen satisfaction is constantly improving.

---

[83] Gavin, Robert, "Getting a Lift – The Rockies Emerge as Pocket of Prosperity in a Slowing Economy", The Wall Street Journal, Wednesday, June 6, 2001.

Improved satisfaction means happy citizens who advertise for the city indirectly — "when asked to note their most recent experience with city employees, residents rated their experience highly when it came to 'feeling valued' and being treated with 'courtesy'"[84].

But Fort Collins isn't the only city in the United States which has realized that improving its image, its attractiveness and its quality of life will improve its financial situation. Fort Collins is one of many cities in the United States which are on the road to recovery. In their book, Comeback Cities, Paul Grogan and Tony Proscio examined this phenomenon. "The American inner city is rebounding—not just here and there, not just cosmetically, but fundamentally. It is the result of a fragile but palpable change in both the economics and the politics of poor urban neighborhoods. Though not yet visible everywhere, the shift is discernible in enough places to unsettle long-standing assumptions about the future of older urban communities."[85]

Joining Fort Collins as a front runner in the race to attract citizens and tax income through a general overhaul of blighted inner-city areas is Chattanooga, Tennessee. With 148,820 (1999) citizens, Chattanooga has seen a sharp increase in population over the last 10 years. "Once a prime example for everything wrong with postindustrial America, Chattanooga is turning itself around. The city's formerly decaying

[84] City of Fort Collins, Colorado, City Scape: A Portrait of Progress-2001 Report to the Community, pg. 6
[85] Grogan, Paul S.; Proscio, Tony, Comeback Cities: A Blueprint for Urban Neighborhood Revival, pg. 1

riverfront is now a thriving entertainment district that draws more than a million visitors a year. Electric buses (locally built and free to ride) ply downtown streets. A not-for-profit group is spending more than $30 million a year on housing and the air, once so dirty you had to drive with your headlights on at noon, is clean again."[86]

Once again, an important factor in turning around the inner–city was to include the residents in the process. The diversity and creativity found within this American inner-city served as a catalyst for creating new ideas for the future of the city. "Many Chattanoogans attribute their success in large part to what is often called "the visioning process" — a series of public meetings in which residents are encouraged to offer their ideas for the future."[87]

Having realized that their ideas were being incorporated into the new concept for the city, the citizens took possession of their neighborhoods and started to care about what happened in them. As a result of all of the positive changes taking place, Chattanooga was featured as a best practice city at the 2nd National Conference on Science, Policy and the Environment at the Smithsonian Museum in Washington, D.C., in 2001.

These same processes were happening simultaneously throughout the United States in cities such as Charleston, South Carolina; Portland, Oregon; Baltimore, Maryland; Boston, Massachusetts; and

[86] Graham, Lamar, "Our Restored Cities, Where the Living is Easier", The Chicago Tribune – Parade Magazine, Sunday, April 25, 1999, pg. 4

[87] ibid., pg. 5

perhaps the most famous of them all in the South Bronx, New York and in New York in general.

The key to what happened in these cities was a change in attitude towards crime and to the environments in which crimes where committed. Being poor didn't necessarily mean one had to live in a dangerous neighborhood. A "Zero-Tolerance" attitude towards crime helped to make even some of the poorest neighborhoods safe for its residents. This "Zero-Tolerance" attitude came about largely through written criticism of the existing law enforcement system through the media and the press, who were mirroring the dissatisfaction of citizens throughout the United States.

An experiment was conducted by Stanford psychologist Philip Zinbaro in 1969, in which two cars were left on city streets–the one intact and the other with a single broken window. Left unattended, the car with the broken window was quickly stripped and destroyed. The other vehicle remained untouched for a week. After the researcher broke a window on the second vehicle, it also was vandalized. Spurned by the insights gained through this experiment, authors James Q. Wilson and George Kelling published an article in the *Atlantic Monthly* magazine in March of 1982 in which the results of Professor Zinbaro's experiment "'broken windows' were used as a metaphor to stand for a set of broader observations about the relationship of all manner of physical disorder and crime on city streets."[88]

[88] Grogan, Paul S.; Proscio, Tony, Comeback Cities: A Blueprint for Urban Neighborhood Revival, pg. 155

Their observations and conclusions changed the form of law enforcement in the United States dramatically and became the catalyst for a new and tougher enforcement of existing laws. "We suggest that untended behavior…leads to the breakdown of community controls. A stable neighborhood of families who care for their houses, mind each other's children and confidently frown on unwanted intruders can change, in a few years or even a few months, to an inhospitable and frightening jungle. A piece of property is abandoned, weeds grow up, and a window is smashed. Adults stop scolding rowdy children; the children, emboldened, become more rowdy. Families move out, unattached adults move in. Teenagers gather in front of the neighborhood store. The merchant asks them to move; they refuse. Fights occur. Litter accumulates. People start drinking in front of the grocery store, in time, an inebriate slumps to the sidewalk and is allowed to sleep it off. Pedestrians are approached by panhandlers."[89]

But the enforcement of existing laws is not the only thing which must happen in order for a reduction of crime to take place in an area. It has been shown that the environment in which crimes are committed also plays a role.

At the time in which the subway system in New York was at its most dangerous it was also in the worst state of repair that it had ever been. Graffiti, vandalism, and fires within the subways caused the entire system to exude an atmosphere of danger and hopelessness. In the mid-1980's the city of New York

---

[89] Kelling, George, and James Q. Wilson, "Broken Windows", Atlantic Monthly, March 1982, pp. 29-38

hired George Kelling as a consultant in an effort to clean up its subways. Kelling suggested a change in management and David Gunn was appointed director. Gunn implemented a multi-million dollar program to renew the system, beginning with the overwhelming physical condition of the infrastructure.

Gunn encountered criticism. Why, so the prevalent theory of the time stated, would you concentrate on cleaning the wagons and the subway stops if there are more important things to do like reducing the number of violent crimes within the system? Gunn disagreed and implemented his plan. As he stated, "The graffiti symbolizes the collapse of the system. If we want a renewal of the system and better employee moral, then we have to win the battle against the graffiti. If we don't win this battle, then all of the management reforms and all of the physical improvements will have been for nothing."[90]

So Gunn implemented a strict clean-up program within the subway system beginning with the number seven line which went from Queens to Midtown-Manhattan. The graffiti was removed from the unpainted cars using paint remover. The painted cars were repainted. Cars with graffiti were never mixed with renovated cars and once a car was renovated it was never allowed to leave the yard with graffiti again.

Gunn recounted a specific incident which illustrates this point. "We had a train yard on 135th street in Harlem where the trains stood overnight. The boys came in the first night in order to paint the train

---

[90] Gladwell, Malcolm, Der Tipping Point, pg. 147

white. They came the following night again, after the white paint had dried, and painted the outlines. On the third night they came in order to color the outlines in. It was a three-day-job. We knew that they were there and we waited until they were finished. Then we went out with our rollers and painted over it. The tears were rolling down their faces, but we painted over the whole thing from top to bottom. We had to make it clear to them. If you want to spend three nights painting the train, fine. But your work will never see daylight."[91]

Gunn spent six years, from 1984 until 1990, improving the physical condition of the subway system in New York. In a second phase of subway renewal, the New York Transit Authority hired William Bratton as chief of the Transit Police. Bratton, a Boston policeman, like Gunn, was a supporter of the "Broken Window Theory" and even called George Kelling his intellectual mentor.

Facing the highest crime rate in its history, Bratton began by cracking down on the fare dodgers and faced the same criticism that Gunn had faced with his anti-graffiti campaign. Bratton chose this point to start because he believed that fare dodging, similar to graffiti, was a sign of chaos that invited further criminality. At the time, it was estimated that approximately 170,000 passengers dodged fares each day. Some of these were youth, others adults. As honest passengers realized that fare dodging brought no retribution, it encouraged them to dodge fares as well. Why pay the fares when others don't and get away with it? The current police theory of the time

[91] Gladwell, Malcolm, Der Tipping Point, pg. 148

regarded fare dodging as a petty crime. The difficulty in prosecuting someone who stole $1.25 outweighed the benefits, so the police thought, and the process wasn't worth the effort spent filling out the paperwork. Unfortunately, this attitude encouraged copycat criminals and the problem exploded.

Bratton started by analyzing the system. He then chose the subway stations in which fare dodging was at its highest and assigned up to ten plainclothes police to these stations. The police at the stations then caught every single fare dodger, put them in handcuffs, and stood them on the subway platforms in a row. This sent a signal to other potential fare dodgers that the Transit Authority Police was now serious about stopping them.

Initially, the enthusiasm of the Transit Police for this new-found prosecutorial vigor was non-existent since the current system required a processing time of about a day for each of the minor infractions. However, what happened then quickly changed the morale of the police force. Bratton converted a bus into a rolling police station reducing the processing time to an hour. Additionally, Bratton required the processed fare dodgers to be checked for other potential criminal activities and the results were astonishing. It turned out that at least one in seven of these fare dodgers was also a wanted criminal for another crime.

Bratton relates, "For the cops, this was a goldmine. Every arrest was a treasure chest. What toy will I get? A Gun? A Knife? Is there an arrest warrant? Is this a murderer?...After a while the dodgers realized what was going on, left the weapons at home, and paid the fares."[92] It wasn't difficult to convince anyone about the necessity of this procedure anymore as the number of felonies within the subway system dropped 75 percent between 1990 and 1994, and the number of robberies by 64 percent within the same time period.

In 1994, William Bratton returned to Boston as superintendent of police. However, in the same year the newly elected Mayor of New York City, Rudolph Giuliani, called him back to New York City where he then had the chance to implement his style of policing city-wide. "As the world now knows, his approach worked the same rapid wonders all over New York. 'Order policing' was applied with a vengeance against the whole spectrum of antisocial behaviors, not only the famous squeegee men…, but also public intoxication and urination, and even playing loud boom boxes in residential neighborhoods after dark…Giuliani and Bratton turned that orthodoxy (don't bother with small crimes, go after the 'serious crimes'– of course after they were committed) on its head by deliberately obsessing over the small stuff. In so doing they transformed the whole environment, which according to Kelling and Wilson was causing the serious crimes to occur in the first place."[93]

Using this new approach to crime fighting and faced with the enforcement on the level of the police commander (only commanders who were committed to double digit crime reduction were promoted and those who did not succeed were fired), homicides

---

[92] Gladwell, Malcolm, Der Tipping Point, pg. 150
[93] Grogan, Paul S., Comeback Cities, pp. 159-160

dropped 70 percent in New York City and major felonies dropped 46 percent. This changed the image of New York and produced the seed for what has become a wonder in American cities. People began moving back into the city and this slowed if not stopped the flight from the city into the suburbs—a long-time cause of urban deterioration.

Taking cue from the successes in New York, Boston and other big cities, the smaller cities, like Chattanooga, followed suit. These also experienced the amazing turnaround of following the "Zero–Tolerance" law enforcement plan coupled with downtown renewals. The subsequent return of former citizens into the city was the result. After having transformed derelict buildings into dwellings for low to moderate income persons; after cleaning up and planting gardens in abandoned properties; after injecting badly needed public interest facilities into the heart of the city (the new Aquarium), the city and the special interest groups transformed the neighborhoods in Chattanooga making it safe for the citizens living there. "Since moving in almost two years ago, she (Janet Richie, a citizen of Chattanooga) has witnessed dramatic changes. On her building's ground floor is a popular tea room. A new jazz club and an antiques center are nearby. The juke joints have been shut down. The porn shop is being gutted. 'Now', says Richie, 'this whole area back to the Aquarium (about 13 Blocks away) is safe for walking.'"[94]

---

[94] Graham, Lamar, "Our Restored Cities, Where the Living is Easier", The Chicago Tribune – Parade Magazine, Sunday, April 25, 1999, pg. 4

The psychological explanation for the effect described above can be found within the realm of Humanistic Psychology. The father of this field of psychology was Dr. Abraham Maslow, who has been mentioned previously and whose work will be examined in depth in the next chapter. Essentially, based upon the research of Dr. Maslow, the need for safety is one of the primary human needs. If a community manages to provide this need, it frees its citizens to concentrate upon other activities, among them, the pursuit of a meaningful existence through relationships and through economic/business activities. By providing one of the most basic human needs, a society can provide the impetus for the location or relocation of independent problem-solvers to it. This will improve a society's standing in light of international competition. Additionally, providing an environment in which the lower human needs are met frees an individual to psychologically progress to higher levels of development.

On the whole, it is once again becoming interesting to live in cities. Singles and young couples without children are realizing the advantages of living within walking distance (or within a mass-transit ride) to libraries, theaters, museums and other cultural attractions. The original appeal of city life is being rediscovered because the new law enforcement approach, and city renewal efforts are slowly diminishing the aspects which made city life unattractive.

One of the last vestiges of the old order are the public school systems in these cities. Having realized that the unattractiveness of the cities' school systems was a major hurdle in convincing young families to move back into cities, the mayors of Chicago, Cleveland and Detroit have personally taken responsibility for their public schools. This is an effort to stem the tide of flight by middle-class families towards the suburbs, these families being the ones who pay proportionally more taxes than other societal groups. By improving the public school systems, the mayors hope that families that loved the amenities of the city but wanted good schools for their children will come back into the city to live.

The mayors hoped and hope to change the encrusted and rusty public school systems by giving the power of choice back to parents. Passing out vouchers to families with children allows those families to choose where they want their children to receive an education. It's free-competition at work, almost guaranteeing that schools in which large numbers of children are being taken out of will have to improve, or cease to exist.

Evidence is mounting that a gradual change in the condition of cities throughout the developed world is taking place and certain investors, who have recognized the trend, are pushing this development and at the same time reaping the rewards of it. Peter Jackson, director of the Oscar-winning *Lord of the Rings* trilogy and of the 2005 *King Kong* remake, single-handedly created a boom in the economy of his hometown of Wellington, New Zealand, by creating one of the world's most sophisticated filmmaking complexes within that city.

"He did it in New Zealand concertedly and by design. Jackson, a Wellington native, realized what many American cities discovered during the '90s:

Paradigm-busting creative industries could single-handedly change the ways cities flourish and drive dynamic, widespread economic change."[95] By providing fertile ground for creativity, Jackson created a unique environment in which that creativity was allowed to flourish, attracting talented and creative people from around the globe. "He realized...that with the allure of the *Rings* trilogy, he could attract a diversely creative array of talent from all over the world to New Zealand: the best cinematographers, costume designers, sound technicians, computer graphic artists, model builders, editors, and animators."[96]

Additionally, in a surprise statement in the summer of 2003, former London mayor Ken Livingstone announced the implementation of a "Zero-Tolerance" crime policy. In Athens, Greece, a group of citizens has joined forces to create a "Broken Window" group, whose purpose is to clean inner-city lots of debris and then make them into mini-parks by planting flowers and shrubbery. The City of Curitiba, Brazil, a shining example of sustainable development also implemented what was, quite possibly, the first example of "Zero-Tolerance" enforcement in 1972.

The Broken-Window theory, which gave birth to the idea of Zero-Tolerance, includes the concept that the physical state of an environment has as much influence on the frequency and seriousness of crimes committed as the amount of potential criminals within the community. Also, normal citizens put in a

---

[95] Florida, Richard, "Creative Class War", Washington Monthly, January 15, 2004, Online: www.alternet.org
[96] ibid.

threatening environment may themselves become criminals purely because of the environment in which they find themselves. Conversely, the renewal of the physical state of the environment in an area which has a high rate of crime will, most probably, cause the rate of crime to decrease. Curitiba did just that in the former city center which had become degenerate and was originally slated for demolition. "At 6:00 on a Friday evening in 1972, an hour after the law courts had closed, the renewal of Curitiba began. City workmen began jack-hammering up the pavement of the central historic boulevard, the Rua Quinze de Novembro. Working round the clock, they laid cobblestones, installed streetlights and kiosks, and planted tens of thousands of flowers. Forty-eight hours later, their meticulously planned work was complete. Brazil's first pedestrian zone—one of the first in the world—was ready for business. By midday Monday it was so thronged that the shopkeepers, who had threatened to sue because they feared lost traffic, were petitioning for its expansion. Some people started picking the flowers to take home, but city workers promptly replanted them, day after day, until the pillage stopped."[97]

Another aspect of community, which an independent problem solver values, is the idea of image. Here a place is valued based upon its authenticity and historic background. Contrary to the United States, most European nations and their former colonies have long recognized the need for the pro-

---

[97] Hawken, Paul; Lovins, Amory; Lovins, L. Hunter; Natural Capitalism, pg. 287

tection of historic buildings and the restoration of the built environment. One needs only to look at the cities in the list of UNESCO World Heritage Sites to recognize that the most of them are located in Europe. By contrast, only one city in the United States has achieved the status of World Heritage Site.

The European Union, after realizing that the quality of the physical environment had a direct effect on the economic development of a city, created the URBAN program in the early 1990's. This program was designed to inject needed investment into the infrastructure of a deteriorated section of a city. Within the parameters of the program social, infrastructural as well as public projects could be funded and the focus of the funding was directed toward regions of the European Union which were economically threatened. The program proved so effective that the European Union repeated it in the financial Frame which followed. The expansion of the European Union in 2004 brought an additional challenge to the economic development of Europe, as the available funding was further stretched to provide new Member States with support, having already been depleted through previous expansions of the Union, including the integration of the former DDR.

New Urbanism Examples

The New Urbanists/ Neotraditionalists, on the other hand, believe in creating new, highly-planned communities using the age-old principles of good community design. These communities can either be entirely new, that is, a greenland site, or located within an existing city. Let's examine some of these communities more closely.

Celebration, a Disney community in Southern Florida was developed based upon an original idea from Walt Disney himself. "It will be a city that caters to the people as a service function. It will be a planned, controlled community, a showcase for American industry and research, schools, cultural and educational opportunities. In EPCOT (Experimental Prototype Community of Tomorrow)...there will be no retirees. Everyone must be employed. One of our requirements is that the people who live in EPCOT must help to keep it alive."[98]

Disney, a master at creating settings, set out to create a setting in which to place his ideal type of person: young, educated, and employed. Although Disney envisioned the creation of the perfect community in the early 1960's, it wasn't until the late 1990's that the first residents moved into the new Disney community. Michael Eisner, Chairman of Disney, noted that: "We looked at what made communities great in our past, added what we've learned from the best practices today, and combined that with a vision and hope for strong communities

---

[98] Thomas, Bob, Walt Disney – An American Original, pg. 349

in the future." He added, "We believe the result will be a very special community."[99]

Celebration, Florida was designed as a year-round community encompassing 4,900 acres of land (residents are required to live in Celebration at least 80% of the year). The core of the community is the central business district which includes a mixture of retail shops, restaurants, offices and apartments. A town hall, post office, grocery store and cinema are also included within this area. The town center is located next to a wide promenade circling a lake in the center of town. Boat rentals, a city park, a pedestrian mall, health facilities, a library, and a public school which has an enrolment of approximately 800 students are located there.

Additionally, the health campus includes, among its services, comprehensive healthcare, advanced diagnostics and a fitness /wellness center.[100] These central core functions are all located within five walking minutes of the single-family homes surrounding it. Beyond the residential areas, a protected band of about 4,700 acres of land surrounds the built-up portion of the community and provides easy access to nature with miles of nature trails running through it. The community also has strict requirements as to the types of homes allowed to be built within it. Included in the available styles of homes are: Victorian, Classical, Colonial Revival, Costal, Mediterranean, and French.

This architectural policy is designed to ensure the compatibility of newly built homes to the existing

[99] www.disneycelebrationfacts.com
[100] ibid.

ones within the community. Homes are required to have oversized porches and verandas that face the streets. This is a feature indicative of New Urbanism developments which ban garages and driveways to an alley behind the house, thus encouraging social interaction between members of the community. Additionally, a feature often criticized by environmentalists, the obligatory par 72 public golf course and a 3-hole junior practice range with clubhouse are also part of the community's amenities.

If one carefully examines the community scheme of Celebration, it quickly becomes apparent that this planning contains many of the same features found in the Industrial Villages and Garden City plans of the past. Among these similarities are: the central town core with functions; a well-organized block structure; single-family home areas facing the street with their porches and verandas; automobiles banned toward the back of properties and into alleys; and close and immediate access to large park and natural areas.

The commercial and planning success of Celebration has caused much international publicity. Additionally, Celebration has also won numerous planning and development awards. Among the first of these was Urban Land Institute's National Award for Excellence in New Community Design otherwise known as the Outstanding New Community of the Year award, which Celebration received on October 5th, 2001.

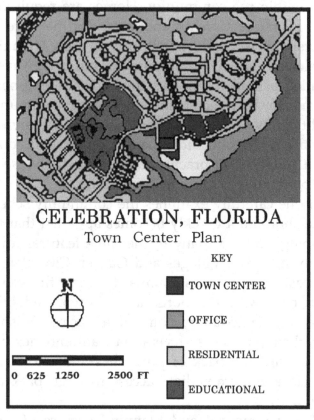

Figure 5. Celebration, Florida, Town Center Plan
Source: Courtesy of Robert A.M. Stern and Associates and Jacquelin Robertson, 2004

Celebration is a full-time community of residential properties designed not only as a place of residence, but also as a place to experience all of the amenities which a more mature community would be able to offer its citizens. As such, this development was groundbreaking—a subdivision development, which was designed and planned like a city and built by a company known for its entertainment venues and products. Featuring many of the amenities and qualities of place desired by the new independent problem-solvers, this town could be viewed as one of the first of its type.

Seaside, Florida, a planned community designed in the early 1980's, is another often sited example of New Urbanism. Seaside, in contrast to Celebration, was originally conceived as a vacation community and although completely planned, the community developed slowly, beginning with a core of 12 homes and corresponding public facilities such as a pavilion, a gazebo, and a small park with garden furniture including a chess pavilion.[101]

The idea of Seaside came after Alabama businessman, Robert Davis, decided to turn his grandfather's "scrubby Golf Coast tract into an architecturally ambitious resort community for enlightened Southerners".[102] To do this he hired two of the most influential New Urbanism architects active in the United States, Andres Duany and Elizabeth Plater-Zyberk, both of which had been mentored by the father of the New Urbanism movement, London-based Leon Krier.

In order to create a cohesive community with a sense of community spirit, the architects chose to model this new community on existing 18th and 19th century Southern American towns. Interestingly enough, these towns themselves were often created following the principles of the Industrial Villages movement of the late 18th century or the Garden City movement of the 19th century. Although never meant to be a real full-time neighborhood, Duany and

---

[101] Mohney, David; Easterling, Keller; Seaside–Making a Town in America, pg. 38

[102] ibid., pg. 42

Plater-Zyberk consciously included qualities in the plan which would aid the development of a real full-time community.

Among these characteristics was the decision to instill a sense of community by implementing an aesthetic code of building. This guideline, similar to the six styles of Architecture available in Celebration, created a sense of community cohesiveness and through this helped develop a sense of community identity. Because Seaside was never intended to become a full-time residential community it lacks many of the traits of a community sought by members of the new independent problem-solvers. However, Seaside does follow a number of the recommendations for Smart Growth communities such as: compact building design; a walkable community (all sections of Seaside can be reached within a five minute walk); a distinctive, attractive community with a sense of place. Seaside is also located in close proximity to nature, with the Golf Coast bordering the community on the one side, and a natural preservation area on the other.

As one can clearly see in Figure 6[103], Seaside developed around a strong central core with the main community functions being located within this core. This is similar to the plans of Celebration, the Industrial Villages, and the Garden Cities of previous centuries. Although primarily a community of single-family vacation homes, Seaside also provides a limited amount of apartments and

---

[103] Mohney, David, ed., Seaside Plan, Miami University Students, 1990, Seaside-Making a town in America, pg. 97

townhouses within the development so that a certain level of economic diversity is included.

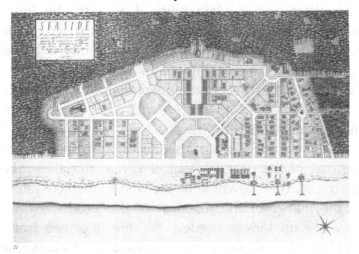

Figure 6. Seaside, Florida, Town Center Plan
Source: Miami University Students, 1990

The creation of planned communities built upon principles and values of a segment of society with increasing influence and financial clout is a new development. Formerly, subdivisions were built primarily with the interests of the developer in mind. Maximizing profits was the highest priority. Now, independent problem solvers are exerting their influence to such an extent, that entire communities are being designed and built according to their moral and ethical ideals. The spread of the idea of New Urbanism is one indicator of the advancement of the values of these increasingly influential members of society. Another indication of the advancing shift in societal ideals is the emergence of an alternative business and development form.

Whereas New Urbanism is an idea which focuses on the design of the built environment, Natural Capitalism and Sustainability deal with the long-term management of a community or society. The predominant form of administration today is based upon the principle of Capitalism. Here, growth is the most important economic aspect and the whole apparatus is built on the idea of creation, consumption, and casting off.

The system is linear and no thought is given to the cost of the procurement of raw materials to the environment as a whole or the cost to the ecosystem of the planet of the disposal of the products once they are no longer needed. 'Where it comes from' and 'where it is going' are irrelevant to the economic equation. Market-driven speculation is forcing some companies to make decisions in order to boost short-term stock prices, but disregard the long-term consequences of those decisions on the environment and on society as a whole.

There is, however, an alternative business and governmental management methodology which is rapidly gaining acceptance throughout the world. This methodology is called Natural Capitalism or Sustainability and it is beginning to take hold in small but decided ways all over the world. In order to examine this phenomenon, it is important to look at a few best-practice examples of implementation. One of the most important of these can be found, contrary to what one might think, in Brazil.

Natural Capitalism/Sustainability Examples

As noted earlier, the authenticity or identity of a place, often characterized by its historic buildings and inherent physical qualities, is only one necessary part in a large range of amenities which a country or city has to offer in order to attract independent problem-solving members of society. Once having provided these amenities, a country or city cannot count on being able to "rest on its laurels". A balance of providing amenities and sustaining them has to be achieved in order to guarantee a long-term economic expansion supported by and initiated through these creative societal members.

Leading researchers in the United States have documented the current trend of flight of Creative Class members of society out of the United States to other countries in the world. "What should really alarm us is that our capacity to...adapt is being eroded by a different kind of competition...as cities in other developed countries transform themselves into magnets for higher value-added industries. Cities from Sydney to Brussels to Dublin to Vancouver are fast becoming creative-class centers to rival Boston, Seattle, and Austin. They're doing it through a variety of means from government subsidized labs to partnerships between top local universities and industry. Most of all, they're luring foreign creative talent, including our own. The result is that the sort of high-end, high-margin creative industries that used to be the United States' province and a crucial source of our prosperity have begun to move overseas. The most advanced cell phones are being made in Salo, Finland, not Chicago. The world's leading airplanes are being designed and built in Toulouse and Hamburg, not Seattle."[104]

An amazing example of long-term sustainable development within cities can be found, contrary to what one might expect, in South America. The city of Curitiba, Brazil has a long history of sustainable development and of providing an incredible range of quality of life amenities for its citizens. As a result, it is one of the most prosperous and well-organized cities in Brazil. This city is such an extraordinary example of sustainable development, that it bears looking at closely.

Curitiba, Brazil
Three decades of thoughtful city planning

Figure 7. Curitiba, Brazil, City Logo
Source: www.curatiba.org

Curitiba was founded in the 17th century as a gold mining camp and became the capital of the State of Paraná in 1856. The city grew rapidly after 1940, with the population expanding threefold within 25 years and swelling to its current size of 1.6 million people. "Though starting with the dismal economic profile typical of its region, in nearly three decades the city has achieved measurably better levels of education, health, human welfare, public safety, democratic participation, political integrity, environmental protection, and community

[104] Florida, Richard, "Creative Class War", Washington Monthly, January 15, 2004, Online: www.alternet.org

spirit than its neighbors, and some would say than most cities in the United States."[105]

How did it accomplish this? In 1965, the city, while grasping the difficulties facing it and in a move unprecedented for its time, created a fully integrated and sustainable planning scheme. The Master Plan had as its main goals "the limitation of central area growth and the encouragement of commercial and service sector growth along two structural north-south transport arteries, radiating out from the city center."[106] Another aim of the Master Plan was "to provide economic support for urban development through the establishment of industrial zones and to encourage local community self-sufficiency by providing all city districts with adequate education, health care, recreation, and park areas."[107]

Additionally, the city created a very unique transportation system based upon a high-speed, high-frequency bus system which moves along the major traffic arteries. Despite the exploding population of the city, Curitiba chose to implement an energy-efficient bus scheme as part of the public transportation instead of a light rail or subway system, which conventional planning would have favored.

Why did Curitiba opt for the bus system? Curitiba chose the transportation system which would offer the most long-term passenger miles with the least amount of economic expenditure. The city subsequently invested the savings in a city-wide

---

[105] Hawken, Paul; Lovins, Amory; Lovins, L. Hunter; Natural Capitalism, pg. 288

[106] http://www.Curitiba, Brazil.htm

[107] ibid.

education system which also included adult further education classes. Thus Curitiba exhibited one of the hallmark traits of both Sustainable Development as well as Natural Capitalism, that is, to create long-term solutions to problems which benefit the greatest number of individuals and the ecosystem instead of solving only one problem and thereby creating a surfeit of new problems in the process.

The respect and conservation of all natural assets is one of the major principles of Natural Capitalism / Sustainable Development and a reoccurring benchmark of the Curitiba Master Plan. Included among the highly respected natural resources is the resource of human capital. Often neglected in the industrialized world with its ever increasing levels of massive unemployment, this extremely valuable asset was integrated within the scope of the Curitiba Master Plan and the result of this change in thinking gives a valuable lesson in respecting the value of human life and creativity.

Curitiba primarily used money saved by reductions in the cost of infrastructure and savings within governmental systems to invest in the education of its citizens. Additionally, Curitiba pursued an aggressive investment in its park and community functions creating an integrated approach to community investment and improving the quality of life characteristics of its city. One of the most interesting of the many examples of the integrated savings and planning methodology used in Curitiba is the creative reuse of the public transportation system throughout the 1.6 million people community.

As noted earlier, the transportation system of Curitiba uses a system of high-speed buses which run at a rapid frequency. "Each lane of express buses carries 20,000 passengers per hour. That's about as many as a subway carries, indeed, it's just like a subway, except that it costs at least 100 times less (tenfold less than a surface train) and can be installed in six months, not a generation."[108] Additionally, 9 different varieties of buses are matched to the needs of riders so that the number of empty seats is reduced.

This convenience coupled with reduced bus fares makes this system of transportation the most popular in Curitiba. Although a high rate of car ownership also exists, owners of the automobiles prefer to leave their cars at home in favor of using the practical public transportation system. Because of the high rate of useage of the public transportation system, the system is self-supporting.

Independent bus companies which are under contract to drive the necessary routes and drive a total of 230,000 bus miles per day (this is the equivalent of a distance of nine times around the world) are able to replace their buses with regularity.[109] This means that the level of service provided to the passengers is increased through the use of the most modern and fitting transportation system available.

But what to do with the old buses, since the average age of the vehicles in service is only 3.5 years old?[110] A Capitalistic solution to the problem would have encouraged the removal and discarding of old buses without giving much thought to the ecological

---

[108] Hawken, Paul; Lovins, Amory; Lovins, L. Hunter, Natural Capitalism, pg. 294
[109] ibid., pg. 294
[110] ibid., pg. 299

impact of this method. Additionally, the cost of throwing the buses away would be ignored. Curitiba examined the whole scope of the problem and created a unique approach to the reuse of this asset.

The old buses, using the principles of recycling prevalent in Curitiba, "often become mobile job-training centers. Parked in the slums and re-outfitted, they are called *Linha do Oficio* ("The Jobs Route" or "The Line to Work"), and staffed by locally recruited, frequently rotated teachers who offer training in more than forty in-demand trades or disciplines to more than 10,000 people a year, mainly on nights and weekends. A three-month course costs only two bus tokens—less than a dollar. Other recycled buses become clinics, classrooms, baby-sitting centers, food markets, soup kitchens, and coaches for weekend excursions in the parks."[111]

The reuse of the buses is only one example of the many ways in which Curitiba sought and still seeks to develop solutions to problems facing the community which have the greatest benefit for the greatest number of citizens. The well designed and integrated bus transportation system is augmented by a number of other transportation options. In addition to individual car ownership, Curitiba offers a highly organized taxi system with over 2,200 taxis. Two-thirds of these taxis are radio dispatched and 90 percent of them are driver-owned.

Bicyclists are also included within the traffic pattern as Curitiba designed and created an integrated system of over 100 miles of bike paths.

---

[111] Hawken, Paul; Lovins, Amory; Lovins, L. Hunter, Natural Capitalism, pp. 299-300

Offered in two levels of difficulty, these bike paths include a level path system for leisurely travel and a hilly path system for bicyclists who prefer a more athletic experience. Other transportation options are available for the members of the community not normally able to participate in community life. "Special buses, taxis, and other services are provided for the handicapped, including travel to 32 specialized schools."[112]

In addition to providing transportation options for handicapped and elderly members of the community, Curitiba also supports an integrated educational system. City planners created a system of local libraries called "Lighthouses of Knowledge". These are tower-like structures located throughout Curitiba, virtually one in each neighborhood. These structures serve to support the literacy of the community as well as to offer a local structure of security, as these towers are illuminated and manned with police, one on each tower. This conjures to mind the function of old city walls in medieval Europe with their watchtowers. As has been discussed previously in this work, creating an atmosphere of safety is one of the most important things that a community can do in order to improve its overall quality of life.

Because of its innovative and sustainable urban solutions, Curitiba won a UNESCO prize for its urban development. In the Curitiba City Center Plan on the next page, the structure of the city can be compared with New Urbanist planning examples included earlier. As is easy to recognize, the city

---

[112] Hawken, Paul; Lovins, Amory; Lovins, L. Hunter, Natural Capitalism, pg. 295

structure is very similar to many other cities in the industrialized world. Curitiba offers a good example of how sustainable urban development or even the principles of New Urbanism can be inserted into existing city structures in order to create environments in which people gladly live.

Additionally, because quality of life issues are the driving decision-making factor in the choice of a city

Curitiba City Plan, City Center

Figure 8. Curitiba, Brazil, City Center
Source: www.Map of The Center of Curitiba – Centro.htm

of residence for the highly creative and economically crucial independent problem solvers, an industrialized city, or even nation, cannot afford to ignore these factors when creating a city master plan or plan of development. However, sustainable development does not only include the husbandry of natural resources and the improvement of the physical environment.

True sustainable development also acknowledges the necessity for the conservation of the most precious of natural resources, that is, human beings. And an obvious way to acknowledge the value of a human spirit is to include human beings in all governmental decision-making processes including the renewal of the built environment. The cited examples of city renewal, that is: Chattanooga, Fort Collins, Boston, New York, and Curitiba have all placed special emphasis on integrating their citizens in the managerial process.

This inclusion underlines the idea that the opinions of citizens of a community are as important as the planning schemes of government employees. Additionally, including the citizenry in governmental decisions made to affect them utilizes their creative problem-solving potential and will, in all likelyhood, offer a far greater and better pool of options from which to chose an optimum solution. Including the public at large in decision-making processes is a sign of respect and regard for their opinions. Shown this amount of respect, the result is that the same measure of respect will be returned.

The present philosophy of economic development in industrialized nations disregards the fundamental fact that all societal innovations have originated from human beings. Wasting a valuable non-renewable resource like the innovative spirit of a human being is almost as criminal as pumping toxic industrial sewage into the waterways of the world.

Chronic unemployment, often in the double digit percentage range, marks one of the most serious issues facing industrialized nations today. This condition is a clear indicaton of a general disregard for the value of the human being and the creative potential of that human being. Capitalism, in a push to achieve more efficiency and higher profits, has made human effort and human work obsolete. Ironically, products may become cheaper, but without work — Who is going to be able to afford those products? The system has an inherent critical flaw which will ultimately cause it to collapse.

As mentioned, postmodern societies in the world have faced a stagnating GNP or, at best, a minimal increase in GNP over the last few decades. This has led to a change in the value system carried by their citizens. The emphasis on economic growth and rising economic wealth has diminished and instead an emphasis on lifestyle issues has taken its place. Although the postmodern societies have reached a level of maturity which has brought with it numerous structural and organization problems, developing nations are just beginning along the pathway of development.

In China and India, two of the most prominent of these countries, values carried by the citizenry most closely resemble those of modern societies. It can, therefore, be anticipated that current industrializing nations will also go through a similar period of maturation. An improvement in the GNP of those countries will ultimately result in a stagnating economy and high levels of unemployment. Therefore, in order to avoid huge numbers of unemployed Chinese and Indian workers, a shift in worldwide social values and social form needs to take place.

2.4 Social Competition and the Coming Golden Age

"In all science, error precedes the truth, and it is better it should go first than last."
Hugh Walpole

Social Competition

One factor in the present and future competition between societies is, of course, the future freedom of citizens to go anywhere, to work anywhere, and to live anywhere. This will become a very real prospect within the next few years. To some extent, this change has already begun.

Additionally, the population of the world is increasingly migrating into cities. For the first time in history, more human beings live in cities than do in rural areas. This brings with it numerous difficulties, not only in terms of planning and logistics, but also in all aspects of social life. Economy of scale works well when providing basic infrastructural features in a community, but works very badly when it comes to helping an individual to socially integrate and flourish.

This means that societies will be facing a number of increasingly difficult challenges in the decades to come. Among these hurdles will be the transformation of economies from ones based upon principles of radical consumption to ones based upon principles of Natural Capitalism. Another difficulty will be the alteration of job markets to include human capital at all levels, instead of supporting a system which promotes the obsolescense of human effort. Taken together, these major changes will drive the world from one in which Capitalism is prevalent; to one in which Inclusivism™ is the predominant social form. Those societies which succeed in making this conversion will reap the rewards. Those that resist this transformation, will not. Driving all of these changes will be the increasing influence of the independent problem solvers and their growing mobility, both physically and economically.

Interestingly enough, the competition between communities is nothing really new. For example, the

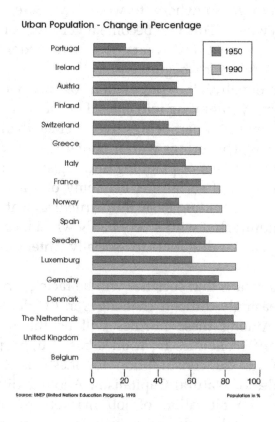

Figure 9. Urban Population Change in Percentages
Source: United Nations Education Program, 1993

tourist authority in Weimar, Germany printed this advertisement in 1910: "WHY is Weimar highly recommended as a seat of residency?...because, despite its size as a medium–sized city, through its theater, museums, art galleries, libraries, archive, monuments and other unique attractions, it offers the inhabitant, in addition to the comforts of a small town, big city pleasures,...**in comparison to cities of the same size it is exceedingly attractive,**...for those seeking knowledge, it has been excellently provided for...the city makes your stay truly enjoyable...it brings diversity in your every day life,...the commercial and material sides of life are also taken into account,...the desire to read is also richly accommodated—and in addition to all of that, it (the city) saves everyone from deadening boredom, and yes, many will be provided with an incomparable benefit and the height of pleasure for the heart and soul, because one will be allowed to live in the light of the observance of the tradition of Goethe."[113] (Translation: author)

So a certain level of competition between cities has always existed. However, in times of increasing levels of birth, this competition is not as life–threatening to cities as the current period of ageing of the population of industrialized nations as well as the mass exodus of people from rural to urban settings is. The only periods within the history of Europe, which are comparable to the current situation, were the periods of plague, the 30 year war, and the time period directly following the influenza

---

[113] Verkehrs- und Verschönerungsverein, "Weimar, Guide to the City", Weimar, 1910

epidemic at the end of the 19th century. These struck some nations in Europe so heavily that it caused certain villages, which had existed up until that time, to cease to exist. Other cities experienced a massive reduction in population.

A primary example of this trend is the current flight of a majority of young people from the new German states into the old German states. Projecting the long-term effects of this flight, it is quite possible that certain "East" German villages or cities will cease to exist within 50 years time. Already, certain former East German cities have had to demolish vast numbers of social housing units in order to avoid having these unpopulated sections of the cities become a social and security problem.

In a similar fashion to the results caused by migration in Germany, a worldwide migration into cities may cause smaller villages throughout the world to be abandoned. In developing nations such as Africa and, more recently, China, the long-term effects of AIDS and HIV will have a similar result, decimating population centers and creating abandoned villages. South American nations are also experiencing the effects of this substantial migration. As a result, many urban centers have had to deal with uncontrolled building in the periphery of the city center and the creation of gigantic slum communities.

In the future, the nations' populations will be concentrated into massive cities worldwide. These cities will be forced to provide a high quality of life for their citizens, if they hope to attract higher-income residents. They will also need to be able to offer a quality of life which will keep those same residents.

Indisputably there are certain cities which now have a higher standing in the world than others. These are cities with a very clear identity and global image that they project. London is clearly one of these World Cities.

Fearing the competition of other World Cities, London commissioned a research project the results of which were published in 1991. "Since the rest of the world shows no sign of sitting back while London grids its resources for the 21st century, it is essential that we know and learn from the competition; that we consider the capital's strengths and weaknesses alongside those of other world cities like New York and Tokyo, alongside major European centers such as Paris, Frankfurt and Berlin."[114]

Within the scope of that research project all factors were considered in the comparison. It was acknowledged that any true comparison between those cities would also have to include factors other than those directly related to economic activity. Among others, these factors were: quality of life factors, social framework factors and environmental factors.

The motivation behind the study was a real fear by London authorities of losing international influence. "On the one hand, New York, Paris and Tokyo are already exploring ways and means of enhancing their positions in the global economy. On the other hand, European cities are trying positively to take

---

[114] Kennedy, Richard, London: World City Moving Into the 21st Century, pg. 3

over London's role as an international center for finance and business, and mounting an assault in the fields of communications, culture and tourism."[115]

London isn't alone in this competitive fear. Paris has also initiated an Ile de France project, the goal of which is to improve conditions within the city in order to lend substance to its claim of being "the economic and cultural capital of Europe". This competition is essential and, like so many things in life, about money. Global cities are usually global exchange points for money. "So world cities are about concentrations of capital and the generation of wealth. But they are also about command and control."[116] Locate a major center of control and exchange of money in a particular city, and that city will quickly establish itself among the ranks of the world cities.

The fact that a city currently has a major role in international finance doesn't necessarily mean that it will always have one. The global network provided through the internet means that these money exchange businesses can locate anywhere. Given the proper business and quality of life factors, it is possible, if not highly likely, that these key businesses will relocate.

One has yet to determine what the long-term effects of the events of September 11th, 2001 will have on the global standing of New York in the economic community. However, safety issues are an important part of quality of life factors. If the international

---

[115] Kennedy, Richard, London: World City Moving Into the 21st Century, pg. 4

[116] ibid., pg. 6

financial community feels that it is no longer safe to locate their offices in New York City, then the probability is very strong that they **will** relocate elsewhere. This will then, in turn, affect the status of New York as a world city.

Additionally, social unrest and the overthrow of dictatorial regimes on a worldwide scale will cause mass migrations of people. These workers will be seeking to improve their quality of life and to flee unstable governmental forms. Ironically, however, those people fleeing from the consequences of a change in government will not be the ones largely responsible for the social unrest and change. As has been mentioned previously, highly-educated and independent problem-solving members of society are the ones who generally instigate social change. Instead, the international refugee workers will more than likely be societal members with fewer skills and abilities.

This will cause conflict between cities and countries. Governments will seek to provide facilities and quality of life amenities in order to attract those highly-educated problem solvers that they need, but will seek to hinder the influx of undereducated socially weak refugee workers, which they do not want. All of this is due to an inherent disregard of the value of the human being as an individual with a unique set of knowledge skills.

So the competition between communities is stiff and the stakes are high and getting higher every day. Luckily, a number of cities have realized that the threat of loss of population and world influence is very real, and they have initiated programs to improve the amenities and quality of life factors within them. On a larger scale, the competition can also be seen to extend to nations.

As has been made abundantly clear in recent times, with events in North Africa leading to massive migrations of refugees into Europe, a long-term international strategy for sustainable development to combat these problems is greatly needed. Only those countries and cities which recognize the current social condition of the world and can develop and implement strategies for attracting and integrating all potential problem-solvers into the social equation will have a real chance at succeeding in the competitive international arena.

Current financial, market and political turmoil might lead to doubt as to the future of cities in particular and world societies in general. However, when one considers the argumentation included here, the picture is not as bleak as it seems. Moreover, the era of a delegation of power to international business conglomerates and the subsequent loss of control by societies to influence their progress as well as the era of an inability, in a number of cases, to influence and control the course of their own development will soon have an end. In its stead, a universal shift in power towards the citizenry and a general movement towards more democracy will take place.

The Society of the Coming Golden Age – The Age of the Independent Problem Solver and Natural Capitalism

The growth in the influence of the independent problem solvers has already begun to change communities worldwide. The realization that the health of our environment is integral to our own health and well-being is one of the primary values of these people, and it has left a mark on every aspect of society. This ideal has driven a number of new developments.

Chief among these is the invention of a number of forms of so-called green-energy. The invention of Fuel-cells and a host of other alternative energy systems have created an enormous foundation upon which to base a new economic expansion. Already, numerous communities worldwide have begun to implement green-energy projects and the application of these technologies is supporting this social metamorphosis.

The country of Germany is another good example of the benefits of embracing this change. As one of the few nations worldwide, Germany recognized the need for these new technologies a number of years ago. The government then embarked upon a methodical course of supporting and underwriting this economic transformation. It provided subsidies to homeowners insulating their houses and encouraged the installation of photovoltaic panels on businesses and homes. This course of action insured that a need for these new products was guaranteed. Germany is currently reaping the rewards for their visionary application of subsidies with a growth of 3%, the highest in the industrialized nations.

Additionally, although Germany, along with many other nations worldwide, had embarked upon a course of unilateral support for the expansion of its nuclear energy producing facilities (against the will of the majority of its citizens); the environmental and nuclear disaster in Japan has caused a radical turn-around in governmental policies. Germany is now the first nation worldwide to make a total and permanent commitment to the transformation of its energy supply from one driven predominantly by fossil fuels to one driven by renewable energy forms.

Once again, Germany has taken the front-runner position in the march toward the new social form of Inclusivism™. This began with the peaceful revolution of 1989 and the reunification of a divided Germany and has continued with ever increasing intensity since then. The push for a stronger regulation of the banking sector and the impetus for more fiscal responsibility of governments worldwide can also be accredited to the German government.

The advancement of the electric motor driven vehicle is another sign of a coming golden age of social prosperity. Coupling electric motor driven vehicles with green-energy is an idea squarely within the principles of Natural Capitalism. Once again, Natural Capitalism is a system in which the entire lifecycle of a product or service is designed so that it brings the greatest benefit both to the user and to the entire ecosystem in which it is used.

Fueled by an increasing need to insure the security of its citizens against a worldwide threat of terrorism, industrialized nations will be forced to reduce their dependency upon foreign oil. Also, the growing force of industrialization in India, China as well as in Asia in general has caused the price of raw materials and fossil fuels to skyrocket. This increase in price of raw materials makes and will make the reuse and sensible use of those raw materials and the weaning off of fossil fuels economically viable.

In the past, a recycling of used and discarded raw materials was not economically viable, as the manufacturing processes were structured solely to convert virgin raw materials into new products. An economic necessity to reuse already existing and discarded raw materials did not exist. The increasing demand for raw materials resulting from the growing industrialization of China, India and Asia in general has changed this economic equation. Subsequently, the postmodern world is being propelled along a course of change in its relationship to the environment and its wasteful use of raw materials. The expected changes in economic structure of these industrialized nations will be all-encompassing; ultimately creating a cleaner, more efficient environment for its citizens and providing quality of life improvements for those citizens.

This push toward the sensible husbandry of all natural resources will lead to a re-evaluation of building construction methods and methodologies. Houses will be refitted with better insulations, with new appliances which use decidedly less energy, with new light bulbs and with new green-energy generating technologies. This will lead to a reduction in the amount of energy required to run these houses. In turn, the reduction in household energy consumption will ultimately lead to the complete weaning of society off of fossil fuel generated electricity.

Combining powerful information technological changes, which have happened in the last 30 years, with an increasing need to expand upon alternative fuel sources as well as to husband natural resources, the coming economy will create an abundance of new occupational opportunities. These occupations will be located in all levels of society ranging from the lowest level worker who will be hired to separate disposable waste from recyclable waste, to the highest level environmental and waste technology expert. This coming boom in new occupational opportunities will generate increased levels of disposable income and perpetuate the boom further. As mentioned previously, this development will then create, many well-to-do people with jobs which they can do anywhere in the world.

This means that societies will be able to count on an increased source of tax income generated by citizens living in the cities as well as businesses located in them, provided that citizens and businesses want to **stay** in that particular city or society. With the competition heating up between individual cities and national governments, these will have to work harder to provide their citizens and businesses with a quality of life standard which will keep them there.

Chapter Three
THOUGHT ALTERATION

The Precursor to Revolution

"Our individual lives cannot, generally, be works of art unless the social order is also." Charles Horton Cooley

It is an undeniable fact that societal units exist to fulfill basic needs. In the animal kingdom, social groupings of animals provide hierarchical structure, defense, life support and organizational structure. It can be argued that the societal units developed by human beings have been created for similar purposes. However, in order to determine if a society is able to fulfill these needs, one must first determine what the intrinsic needs of a human being are.

By examining the historical development of urban units, a picture of the requirements of previous societies can be made. In order to develop the most accurate representation of these needs, it is best to begin by investigating the earliest known forms of these entities. Historical theory suggested that cities were created with a desire for common defense after agricultural surplus led to the possibility of a specialization of skills.

However, this does not explain the fact that some of these same cities continued to exist long after these initial defense issues where resolved. Other experts claim that cities were founded as a central place for economic interaction. This theory forms, in part, the current accepted archeological explanation of city development and is based, in part, on the discovery of the world's oldest known city to date, Çatal Hüyük in Anatolia.

In 1961, British archeologist James Mellaart discovered the city while searching for the parent civilization of a highly developed Neolithic farming village dated to about 6,000 B.C.. [117] What he found,

Çatal Hüyük / Schematic Reconstruction

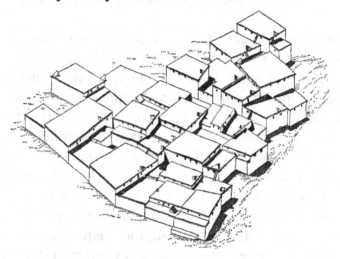

Figure 10. Çatal Hüyük, Neolithic town in Anatolia
Source: Mellaart, James, Catal Hüyük, A Neolithic Town in
Anatolia, 1967, pg. 62

instead of another more highly developed farming village, was a highly developed city, one of the oldest discovered to date. This city was at least 1000 years older than the village (7,000 – 6,000 B.C.), which was proven to be the source of civilization documented in the younger farming village. This discovery turned the prevalent theory of community development on its head and proved that Neolithic

---

[117] Mellaart, James, Catal Hüyük, A Neolithic Town in
Anatolia, 1967, pg. 62

communities had agriculture as well as specialized labor.

Through intensive study of the archeological site, Mellaart discovered that an active trading network was the backbone of the community. This network spanned many kilometers in all directions into the surrounding countryside. The entire community was designed with communal defense in mind. Primary among these defensive features was the total lack of doors into the various dwelling areas from the outside. Dwelling and communal areas were entered by climbing into holes using ladders. Likewise, the main walking areas—terraces, were reached from the outside ground level by ladders leaned against the exterior walls of the community. Without larger openings to the unprotected outside areas, this system provided the maximum level of security for its citizens.

Jane Jacobs, one of the most noted urbanists of the previous century, based her theory that the earliest form of civilization was not a farming community, but a city, upon the discovery of Çatal Hüyük. Taking the most current and scientifically supported of recent theories based upon archeological evidence, the status of the city within human culture is then raised to an even higher level than generally acknowledged. Jacobs, in her book The Economy of Cities, suggested that farming villages were created in order to support the cultural development of the cities which, in turn, supported the advancement of the agricultural communities through innovation and developments in agricultural methods and technology.[118] This means that mankind can be thought of as a race of city dwellers and not, as generally thought, as a race of rural dwellers forced into cities. This provides all the more reason to closely examine the symbiotic nature of the relationship between mankind and its cities.

Additionally, historical differences exist within different cultures as to the form of the cities themselves. Even in the most rural areas, the European tradition created a common central gathering of habitats with surrounding farming acreage. This was also the case in North America as the initial settlers to the continent created central communities with the supporting farmland acreage surrounding them. It wasn't until the Industrial Revolution and the pioneer expansion into the frontier of North America created a single settler mentality, that this historic pattern was broken.

Today, the United Nations suggests that "societies (or cities) have many goals—to ensure the well-being of its present citizens and a better future for the next generation in terms of good health, housing, education, and prosperity, justice for all, the extension of personal freedom, and the maintenance of domestic and external peace."[119]

One can simplify that notion and suggest that even the smallest social form, that is, a single-family unit had and indeed still has a vital purpose in society in general. A society and societal unit has as its prime purpose the creation of conditions which in-

---

[118] Jacobs, Jane, The Economy of Cities, pp. 19-31
[119] United Nations, World Economic and Social Survey 2002, pg. 135

sure the continuation of itself. That is to say that a society exists to provide a framework for producing healthy well-adjusted human beings that in turn produce more healthy well-adjusted human beings. The production of generations of healthy well-adjusted human beings insures the continuation of society in general.

It could be argued that this system falls under the rubric of preservation of species, but one only needs to examine the population development of most European nations generally, and of Italy and Germany specifically, to realize that self-preservation is not something which can automatically be taken for granted. A society can only exist on a long-term basis and grow to its fullest potential, when the number of healthy well-adjusted members vastly exceeds all other groups within it and societal conditions support the success of this group.

A cursory glance at any international news venue will make abundantly clear that the current state of affairs in the world indicates a serious problem in the world's social health. Suicide bombers; rogue gunmen gunning down innocent civilians; violent family clashes ending in injuries and murders; children wielding weapons in schools and killing both classmates and teachers; high-profile pedophile groups and individuals openly claiming that their form of "love" is valid and legitimate; a growth in the number of child abductions and missing children; an exponential increase in the number of and severity of child pornography placed in open internet forums; a huge increase in the number of divorced households and a considerable increase in the number of single households all indicate that worldwide social conditions have deteriorated.

In the business and public arena the indicators of a social collapse are also prevalent. Politicians who plagiarize other's works; national leaders who are willing to gun down their own people in order to maintain power; other leaders who refuse to yield power when voted out of office; businessmen who have no qualms pursuing fraudulent business deals and cheating customers out of enormous sums of money; and a total moral meltdown in the commercial and governmental sector support the idea that a worldwide social deterioration has infiltrated all segments and aspects of society.

When viewing these circumstances, it quickly becomes obvious that something is seriously awry with communities' and governments' ability to provide an environment in which the basic needs of its citizens can be met. Therefore, the first step in rectifying this situation is to be clear on what those needs are. Having determined what the requirements are in order to support the development of healthy individuals, a society can then set about creating a framework for this support.

3.1 The Healthy Human Being

"It is no measure of health to be well adjusted to a profoundly sick society." Jiddu Krishnamurtti

Starting in the 1930's, the clinical and experimental psychologist, Abraham H. Maslow, spent his lifetime examining the fundamental basic human needs and ultimately examining people whose needs had or hadn't been fulfilled over the span of a lifetime. In his groundbreaking work Motivation and Personality from 1956, Maslow postulated that a chronic lack of basic human needs will cause illness in a human being. This means, that the lack of fulfillment of those needs would produce the antithesis of a healthy well-adjusted member of society.

"It is such considerations as these that suggest the bold postulation that a man who is thwarted in any of his basic needs may fairly be envisaged simply as a sick man. This is a fair parallel to our designation as sick of the man who lacks vitamins or minerals. Who will say that a lack of love is less important than a lack of vitamins? Since we know the pathogenic effects of love starvation, who is to say that we are invoking value questions in an unscientific or illegitimate way, any more than the physician does who diagnoses and treats pellagra or scurvy?"[120] Additionally: "We know already that the main prerequisite of healthy growth is gratification of the basic needs. (Neurosis is very often a deficiency disease, like avitaminosis.)"[121] A healthy human

---

[120] Maslow, A.H., Motivation and Personality, pp. 105-106
[121] Maslow, A.H., Toward a Psychology of Being, pg. 163.

being could also be in danger of becoming "unhealthy" or sick if societal conditions deteriorate to the point of creating an environment in which his needs are chronically thwarted.

Dr. Maslow was able to observe many cases, where this lack of fulfillment of needs actually caused physical and mental illness. "I have seen a few cases in which it seemed clear to me that the pathologies (boredom, loss of zest in life, self-dislike, general depression of the bodily functions, steady deterioration of the intellectual life, of tastes, etc.)...were produced in intelligent people leading stupid lives in stupid jobs. I have at least one case in which the appropriate cognitive therapy (resuming part-time studies, getting a position that was more intellectually demanding, insight) removed the symptoms."[122] Further: "I have seen *many* women, intelligent, prosperous, and unoccupied; slowly develop these same symptoms of intellectual inanition. Those who followed my recommendation to immerse themselves in something worthy of them showed improvement or cure often enough to impress me with the reality of the cognitive needs."[123]

So a human being requires an environment in which his basic needs are likely to be met and a societal system which allows him the freedom to pursue individual interests. Provided with this environment, the person then has the greatest possibility of being and staying physically, emotionally and psychologically healthy. Therefore, a healthy human being, the person most "fully human" is one whose

---

[122] Maslow, A.H., Motivation and Personality, pg. 95
[123] ibid., pg. 96

basic needs are gratified, if not completely, then at least to a degree in which they cease to be of foremost importance.

With his basic needs taken care of, a healthy human being is then able to develop his unique and personal abilities to the fullest. "If I were permitted this usage, I should then say simply that a healthy man is primarily motivated by his needs to develop and actualize his fullest potentialities and capacities. If a man has any other basic needs in any active, chronic sense, he is simply an unhealthy man. He is as surely sick as if he had suddenly developed a strong salt hunger or calcium hunger."[124]

Healthy human-beings are individuals that are completely at peace and at rest within themselves. They have no pathological deficiencies or urges. Their only pressing desire is to be able to explore all of their innermost, intrinsic capabilities and then to seek fulfillment through them. Through their position of inner health and strength, these people ultimately have great influence on their surroundings. They support altruistic causes and are willing to make personal sacrifices in order to further these causes.

An unhealthy, or not yet fully developed human being is one who is not at rest within himself. This person is always seeking, yearning for and desiring something. When the person obtains that object of desire, the inner unrest resumes. There is normally no pause, no true lasting happiness which satisfies the never-ending circle of want. An unhealthy individual is a selfish individual, whose personal

---

[124] Maslow, A.H., Motivation and Personality, pp. 105-106

needs and wants are always placed above the needs of others.

A society which is comprised of a majority of selfish individuals, or one in which the people holding power and authoritative positions are inherently selfish, cannot sustain itself and flourish. It is prone to all manners of social unrest and difficulties and will ultimately collapse. Societies which wish to succeed in the long-term must seek to increase their number of healthy, well-adjusted members.

Therefore, the ultimate goal of a society which seeks to increase the number of its members who are healthy or fully-human should be to create conditions conducive to improving the general health of its members. As discussed above, these conditions include providing a social framework in which to assure that the basic human needs are gratified. By providing an environment to encourage the development of these healthy members of society, society in turn benefits from their innovational energy which ultimately fosters a better society for all. Once again, a healthy human being is one who is at rest within himself. They are capable of creating solutions which benefit not only themselves, but also others around them. "...I have found that if I select psychologically healthy humans what they like is what human beings will come to like. Aristotle is pertinent here: 'What the superior man thinks is good, that is what is really good.'"[125]

Society then gains better-equip members who in turn produce better results or innovations through

[125] Maslow, A.H., The Farther Reaches of Human Nature, pg. 9

their work and support society within the scope of international competition. This is becoming increasingly important due to the fact that, as discussed previously, competition between societies, nations and cities is increasing exponentially.

"All other things being equal, we may expect the scientist (or artist, or machinist, or executive, etc.) who is happy, secure, serene and healthy to be a better scientist (or artist, or machinist, or executive, etc.) than if he were unhappy, insecure, troubled, and unhealthy. The neurotic person distorts reality, makes demands upon it, imposes premature conceptualizations upon it, is afraid of the unknown and of novelty, is too much determined by his interpersonal needs to be a good reporter of reality, is too easily frightened, is too eager for other people's approval, etc.

There are at least three implications of this fact. First of all the scientist (or better, truth seeker in general) ought to be psychologically healthy rather than unhealthy to do his best work. Secondly, it may be expected that as a culture improves, thereby improving the health of all its citizens, truth seeking should improve, and third, we should expect that psychotherapy would improve the individual scientist in his individual function."[126]

---

[126] Maslow, A.H., Motivation and Personality, pp. 11-12

Providing an environment in which the individual is able to meet his intrinsic needs is the first step on the road toward creating a society where the majority of citizens are healthy, both physically and psychologically. Healthy and well-developed citizens, in turn, are better able to cope with their environments. In this current time of social, economic, political and environmental unrest, the effects of a non-provision of basic human needs is evident.

Placed in a stable and well-functioning environment, migrants and refugees from international centers of economic and political unrest should begin to heal. Even in societies where there is no obvious external sign of social unhappiness (riots, etc.) the evidence of a serious underprovision of the basic human needs can be found in the increase in the level of crime, domestic violence and in the number of suicides.

To a society or a community which embarks upon a path towards re-creating its social structure, the ultimate reward of this course of action will be a reduction in crime, in health care costs and the creation of better solutions to pressing problems by these citizens. In the long-term, economic prosperity will result as well.

The provision of these basic needs is, therefore, an investment that a society can make in its economic future and in its level of competitiveness. However, this requires an intimate knowledge of human beings and the needs of a human being. Ultimately, the political recognition of this necessity and of the necessity of implementation is the final requirement in order to make a positive impact on societal conditions.

3.2 The Basic Human Needs

"Man is a wanting animal and rarely reaches a state of complete satisfaction except for a short time. As one desire is satisfied, another pops up to take its place. When this is satisfied, still another comes into the foreground, etc. It is a characteristic of the human being throughout his whole life that he is practically always desiring something."[127]
Abraham Maslow

Beginning in his work <u>Motivation and Personality</u>, Dr. Maslow sought to define the basic human needs which must be gratified in order to insure the continued physical and mental health of people within a society (healthy human being/ good person). In ranking order these categories of needs are:

1. Physiological Needs—these are the bodily needs of a human being such as food, shelter, clothing, etc.

2. Safety Needs—these are needs which primarily strive to protect the gratification of physiological needs: safety from crime, secure income, secure housing. This level can also be expanded to include securing the following.

3. Belongingness and Love Needs—these are the need for love and affection, for finding a group in which one fits in, and for finding a mate or partner.

4. Esteem Needs—these needs can be subdivided into two groups. First of all, the desire for strength, achievement, adequacy, mastery and competence, for confidence in the face of the

---

[127] Maslow, A.H., Motivation and Personality, pg. 69

world and for independence and freedom, build one group of esteem needs. The other group consists of the desire for reputation or prestige, for status, dominance, recognition, attention, importance, or appreciation.

5. The Need for Self-Actualization—this need is essentially the fulfillment of one's destiny or life's calling (for lack of a better term). It is the search of each individual for the meaning of his or her life and the desire for self-fulfillment. This tendency can be described as the desire to become more and more of what one is capable of becoming, that is, fulfilling more and more of one's personal potential.[128]

Maslow's Hierarchy of Needs

Figure 11. Maslow's Hierarchy of Needs
Source: Abraham Maslow's Hierarchy of Needs in Personality Synopsis
at ALLPSYCH Online.htm

---

[128] Maslow, A.H., Motivation and Personality, pg. 93.

Interestingly enough, the ranking of these needs occurs necessarily as the first needs must at the very least be partially gratified in order for the needs which follow to be satisfied. However, it is not necessary for all of a lower level need to be satisfied before a higher level need emerges. "Most members of our society who are normal are partially satisfied in all their basic needs and partially unsatisfied in all their basic needs at the same time...For instance, if I may assign arbitrary figures for the sake of illustration, it is as if the average citizen is satisfied perhaps 85 percent in his physiological needs, 70 percent in his safety needs, 50 percent in his love needs, 40 percent in his self-esteem needs, and 10 percent in his self-actualization needs."[129]

With the first need satisfied to a great extent, the next need emerges gradually and unconsciously takes the first need's place as a perceived priority. Therefore, a person who is homeless and hungry most of the time will consider all of the following needs to be unimportant and superfluous. Who needs love if they're starving? "In general, where there are two lacks to be gratified, the more prepotent, i.e., the "lower", is chosen to be gratified."[130]

We need only to look at history to see an affirmation of Dr. Maslow's theories. In all of the great civilizations of ancient times the fulfillment of the lower needs lead to the desire for the higher needs and to the ultimate self-actualization of their

---

[129] Maslow, Abraham H., Motivation and Personality, pp. 100-101.

[130] Maslow, A.H., The Farther Reaches of Human Nature, pg. 146

people. This can be seen in the ancient Egyptian, Greek and Roman cultures to name but a few. The reverse process is equally true, that is to say, if a civilization loses the ability to provide the lower needs, a general pursuit of the higher needs within the society will disappear as well.

This tendency can also be documented in the modern age where periodic economic crises lead to a reduction in the amount of social services and charitable organizations. The support of others who are less fortunate is more probable when most people don't have to fear the loss of their own job as well their source of income and sustenance, that is to say, when the others *truly are* less fortunate. With a loss of job security, which is translated into the loss of economic security, the focus of a human being's goal of needs satisfaction shifts from the higher needs of self-actualization, esteem and love and belongingness, to the lower needs of safety and physiological needs. Coming out of an economic downturn, a society or an individual will once again pick up the needs that it dropped during the process of shedding "unnecessary needs", which was applied in order to facilitate survival.

It is possible, therefore, to determine the level of development of an individual by recognizing the need which currently holds the highest priority for that person. People who are starving are not going to be very interested in going to the opera. People who live in a society where crime is rampant and they have to fear for their lives every day are not going to spend very much time painting works of art.

This same effect applies to group behavior as well. If enough people are gathered together who are all at the same developmental level, a tipping point is reached and the group begins to have the same values and exhibit the same characteristics as the majority of individuals. Here, once again, the effect is reciprocal. If enough individuals reach a certain level of development, then society begins to act according to the values at that level. However, if outside circumstances force a society into a lower level value system, then the individual will, in most cases, also begin to exhibit behavior in keeping with the values of that level.

An individual and its environment are in symbiosis. Should a society improve quality of life aspects, then an individual living within that society will also being to improve their psychological and social quality of life. Should an individual, on the other hand, begin upon a course of self-reflection and inner-psychological development, then this will inevitably have an effect on the environment in which this individual lives.

The basic human needs serve as a benchmark to determine the developmental level of a society or city. Governments, non-governmental organizations and international help agencies can establish the needs level at which a society currently finds itself and will then be able to best utilize funding to move the society along the needs pyramid.

Likewise, this benchmark also applies to an individual. Although an individual can embark upon an inner-psychological pathway by means of two different roadmaps, the ultimate outcome is the same. Psychologists can support the mental health and healing of their patients, if they recognize where along the developmental pathway their patients are.

Using this knowledge they can then determine which psychological maturation steps are necessary to bring their patients to the next developmental level. Patients, themselves, can help their own development by recognizing their location upon the ladder and embracing the opportunity to move higher.

The Basic Human Needs model can also be used to better manage and lead groups. Once having recognized the needs level in which the group currently finds itself, a leader can then determine which steps need to be undertaken, if any, to move the group as a whole to the next psychological level. Here, however, it is important to balance the wishes and goals of the leader against the needs of the individual within the group. For example: a leader of a bank might think that a bank full of level four employees will bring the most profit, however, a radically level four banker might create a financial model which brings the bank a huge profit, but sends the rest of the world into a gigantic economic crisis.

It is, perhaps, most prudent if each individual (and subsequently each society) seeks to achieve the highest level of personal psychological development that they can. Once having reached level five, the perspective becomes so radically different, that a return to old mental and behavioral patterns is not possible. This can only lead to good.

3.3 The Self–Actualized Person

"...we can pick the best specimens of the human species, people with all the parts proper to the species, with all the human capacities well developed and fully functioning, and without obvious illnesses of any kind, especially any that might harm the central, defining, sine qua non characteristics. These can be called "most fully human".[131] Abraham H. Maslow

Having fulfilled the greatest portion of his basic physiological needs, the healthy human being is then able to concentrate on reaching the fullest of his or her potential. Dr. Maslow termed this "self-actualizing". "So far as motivational status is concerned, healthy people have sufficiently gratified their basic needs...so that they are motivated primarily by trends to self-actualization."[132] Maslow then went on to define self-actualization as a constant upgrading of a person's talents, capabilities, potentials and talents. A person who is self-actualized (according to Maslow), is one who has a more encompassing knowledge of his fate, destiny, or vocation. He is a person who accepts his own intrinsic nature and believes that he is on a path of total synergy or integration with his own spirit.

This does not, of course, mean that all people will find themselves at the same level of personal development or in their personal needs. Just as different children in the same classroom learn to read at a speed based upon their personal abilities, so

---

[131] Maslow, A.H., Toward a Psychology of Being, pg. 171.
[132] Maslow, Abraham H., Toward a Psychology of Being-
Second Addition, pg. 25

human beings will move along the needs hierarchy based upon their own personal maturity.

This process, however, can occur at any age. "People can live at various levels in the motivation hierarchy,...they can live barely at the level of survival in the jungle, or they can live in an Eu-

---

Characteristics of Healthy People

- Superior perception of reality
- Increased acceptance of self, others and nature
- Increased spontaneity
- Increase in problem-centering
- Increased detachment and desire for privacy
- Increased autonomy and resistance to enculturation
- Greater freshness of appreciation and richness of emotional reaction
- Higher frequency of peak experiences
- Increased identification with human species
- Changed (the clinician would say, improved) interpersonal relations
- More democratic character structure
- Greatly increased creativeness
- Certain changes in value system

Figure 12. The Characteristics of Healthy People
Source: Maslow, A.H., Toward a Psychology
of Being, pp. 25-26

---

psychian society with good fortune and with all the basic needs taken care of so that they can live at a higher level and think about the nature of poetry or mathematics or that kind of thing."[133]

---

[133] Maslow, A.H., The Farther Reaches of Human Nature, pg. 239

People who have reached the Self-Actualization level of development have traveled through the lower levels of development which are based upon a "me" mentality. In level one the thought is how "I" can get food, clothing, and shelter. At level two the idea is how "I" can secure that which "I" have achieved. In level three a human being seeks to gain love and belongingness for "himself" and in level four the respect and esteem of others for what "I" have achieved is sought.

Between level four and level five, however, something very interesting happens. At level five the individual realizes that "he" is no longer alone in the world and that "his" actions will affect not only "himself" but also others and the environment as well. The "me" mentality changes to a "me-in-we" mentality and the individual recognizes that he is intertwined both with the rest of humanity and with the earth that he inhabits.

It is the first level of human psychological development which is not based upon an inherent idea of selfishness. It is also the first level of development at which, once achieved, the person will not fall back down to a lower level if environmental circumstances change. The change in mentality is so radical, and the thought processes of the individual transform so completely that once transformed, there is no going back. A level five person is a totally different animal.

Unfortunately, this fundamental change brings difficulties with it. As the thought processes of a level five individual are totally different from the other four levels of development, an individual at this level is often viewed as peculiar. Additionally,

Characteristics of Being / Values of Being (B-Values)

1. **Truth**: honesty; reality; (simplicity; essentiality; clean and unadulterated completeness).
2. **Goodness**: (rightness; desirability; oughtness; justice; benevolence; honesty); (we love it, are attracted to it, approve of it).
3. **Beauty**: (rightness; form; aliveness; simplicity; richness; wholeness; perfection; completion; uniqueness; honesty).
4. **Wholeness**: (unity; integration; tendency to oneness; interconnectedness; organization; structure; order, not dissociated; synergy, homonomous and integrative tendencies).
4a. **Dichotomy-transcendence**: (acceptance, resolution, integration, or transcendence of dichotomies, polarities opposites, contradictions); synergy (i.e., transformation of oppositions into unities, of antagonists into collaborating or mutually enhancing partners).
5. **Aliveness**: (process; not-deadness; spontaneity; self-regulation; full-functioning; changing and yet remaining the same; expressing itself).
6. **Uniqueness**: (idiosyncrasy; individuality; noncomparability; novelty; nothing else like it).
7. **Perfection**: (nothing superfluous; nothing lacking; everything in its right place; unimprovable; just-rightness; just-so-ness; suitability; justice; completeness; nothing beyond).
7a. **Necessity**: (inevitability; it must be *just* that way; not changed in any slightest way; and it is good that it *is* that way).
8. **Completion**: (ending; finality; justice; it's finished; no more changing of the Gestalt; fulfillment; *finis* and *telos*; nothing missing or lacking; totality; fulfillment of destiny; cessation and completion of growth and development).
9. **Justice**: (fairness; oughtness; suitability; architectonic quality; necessity; inevitability; disinterestedness; nonpartiality).
9a. **Order**: (lawfulness; rightness; nothing superfluous; perfectly arranged).
10. **Simplicity**: (honesty; nakedness; essentiality; abstract, unmistakability; essential skeletal structure; the heart of the matter; bluntness; only that which is necessary; without ornament, nothing extra or superfluous).
11. **Richness**: (differentiation; complexity; intricacy; totality; nothing missing or hidden; all there; "nonimportance"; ie., everything is equally important; nothing is unimportant; everything left the way it is, without improving, simplifying, abstracting, rearranging).
12. **Effortlessness**: (ease; lack of strain, striving, or difficulty; grace; beautifully functioning).
13. **Playfulness**: (fun; joy; amusement; gaiety; humor; exuberance; effortlessness).
14. **Self-sufficiency**: (autonomy; independence; not-needing-anything-other-than-itself-in-order-to-be-itself; self-determining; environment-transcendence; living by its own laws; identity)."

Figure 13. The B-Values of Self-Actualizing People
Source: Maslow, A.H., The Farther Reaches of Human Nature, pp. 133-135

people who have reached level five development will often suffer mistreatment from individuals at a lower level of development, especially if these hold positions of authority over them.

This is because a lower level individual will view the thought processes of a level five person as a threat to "their way of life". A thought process in which the needs of others feature as great a part in the decision making process as the desires of the individual constitutes a radical departure from the "self" driven philosophy of the lower levels. This is something that a lower level person cannot understand.

There are, generally speaking, two ways in which a person can reach the fifth Maslovian level of psychological development. The first method, as has been discussed, is by having society provide an environment conducive to furthering the psychological growth of an individual. If an individual grows up or lives in an environment in which the basic human needs are provided for, or where an individual does not face undo difficulties providing for his needs, then this frees up energy for personal development. The second manner is far more interesting and unique.

It is normal for people to face periods of challenge in their lives. For most people, these trials lead to a retreat into lower levels of behavior and needs gratification. In some cases, however, the life of the individuals has been so dramatically shaken by this traumatic experience, that it causes them to embark upon a course of inner reflection and inner discovery.

Old behavioral patterns and values are questioned and the person begins to reflect upon the motivations driving them. Quite often, during this period of self-discovery and inner-reflection, an individual will begin to examine spiritual matters and delve into religions and religious philosophies. This is not to be viewed as strange or wrong. A level five individual is a spiritual individual. Spiritual individuals have moved beyond the idea that the world revolves around them. Therefore, the idea of grasping and accepting God is a natural progression from a selfish perspective, to one in which the individual is integrated into a larger more universal fabric.

The march of mankind toward a higher level of psychological development is supported by both of these methodologies. Either through societal advancement or through a course of inner-reflection, an individual embarked upon this journey will ultimately end up at the fifth level of psychological development, or higher. Both approaches are creating increasing numbers of level five society members.

As was discussed previously, the values of society are changing. This was clearly shown within the European Value Systems Survey and examined in depth by Dr. Ronald Inglehart. A generational change is bringing with it a growth in the number of level five individuals. This body of research indicates that society is fast approaching a tipping point. When the number of level five members of society is sufficient, this will cause society as a whole to begin to act in a level five manner. A social revolution is eminent.

3.4 The Healthy Society

"The trouble with the rat race is that even if you win, you're still a rat." Lilly Tomlin

The healthy society is, therefore, one which fulfills the basic needs of human beings allowing them to "self-actualize" and to become most fully human, to use a term from Dr. Maslow. The symbiotic relationship between man and his society must then be examined: "If we were to use the word sick in this way, we should then also have to face squarely the relations of man to his society. One clear implication of our definition would be that (1) since a man is to be called sick who is basically thwarted, and (2) since such basic thwarting is made possible ultimately only by forces outside the individual, then (3) sickness in the individual must come ultimately from a sickness in the society. The good or healthy society would then be defined as one that permitted man's highest purposes to emerge by satisfying all his basic needs."[134]

What benefit does a healthy society gain from these "healthy" people? Obviously, society gains the benefit that these people stay and have children to carry the society further. Additionally, "healthy" or self-actualizing people are the people in society who generally produce the newest innovations; who run the most innovative businesses; who are the most active both socially and politically and who are most creative members of such a society and therefore the society's most valuable members.

---

[134] Maslow, A.H., Motivation and Personality, pp. 105-106

A society which creates an atmosphere in which innovation flourishes (self-actualization) can be assured of future financial and social security in comparison with "bad" societies which hinder such innovation. "It is now quite clear that the actualization of the highest human potentials is possible — on a mass basis —only under 'good' conditions.' Or more directly, good human beings will generally need a good society in which to grow."[135]

Therefore the development or attraction of self-actualizing people requires that a society provide the necessary framework in which these people can flourish. This does not mean that one group or class of societal members be supported to the exclusion of the others, as is sadly so often the case throughout the world today. Instead, the alteration of a societal framework in order to create an environment in which creativity and innovation flourish will only bring advantages for the entire population, regardless at which level of psychological development they find themselves. "There is a kind of a feedback between the Good Society and the Good Person. They need each other; they are sine qua non to each other...It is quite clear that they develop simultaneously and in tandem. It would in any case be impossible to achieve either one without the other...To clarify, it is now clear that with the goodness of the person held constant, it is possible to make social arrangements that will force these people into either evil behavior or into good behavior...to some extent the goodness or badness of a person depends upon

[135] Maslow, A.H., The Farther Reaches of Human
Nature, pp. 7-8

the social institutions and arrangements in which he finds himself."[136]

The world has become a place in which the individual is increasingly becoming independent from his roots, that is to say, that the basic necessary human needs can be fulfilled independently of one's homeland. People are increasingly actively choosing their homeland. In light of this development, one might argue that a successful societal form is one which provides the basic human needs and ultimately allows the individual to develop himself or herself to the fullest, regardless of background or cultural or religious heritage.

This means that a fundamental paradigm shift must take place. Where politicians once perceived citizens as spoiled children, these same politicians must now realize that by providing citizens with what they need, not just what they want, they can ensure that society in general will also reap benefits. A classic win-win situation created from the current win-lose perception of society. "We can now reject the almost universal mistake that the interests of the individual and of society are of necessity mutually exclusive and antagonistic, or that civilization is primarily a mechanism for controlling and policing human instinctoid (sic) impulses ([137]). All these age-old axioms are swept away by the new possibility of defining the main function of a healthy culture as the fostering of universal self-actualization."[138]

---

[136] Maslow, A.H., The Farther Reaches of Human
   Nature, pp. 19-20
[137] Marcuse, H., Eros and Civilization. Beacon, 1955.
[138] Maslow, Abraham H., Toward a Psychology of Being-
   Second Addition, pg. 159

Dr. Maslow suggested that an inherent benefit to society exists through the creation of "good" jobs or "good" working conditions as part of a greater goal to enable self-actualization. By providing these types of working conditions, society will create conditions in which its members inherently move toward the highest human ideals, that is, the B-Values. "There is some evidence to indicate that what we call 'good' jobs and 'good' working conditions on the whole help to move people toward the B-Values; e.g., people in less desirable jobs value safety and security most, while people in the most desirable jobs most often value highest the possibilities for self-actualization."[139]

In this chapter, the benefits to society for providing the basic human needs have been examined. But what effects can be expected if basic human needs are disregarded, ignored or even thwarted by a society? Dr. Maslow gave an accurate if sometimes terrifying view of that type of society: "a dishonest world, an evil world, an ugly world, a split, disintegrated world, a dead, static world, a world of clichés and stereotypes, an incomplete, unfinished world, a world without order or justice, an unnecessarily complicated world, an over-simplified, overabstract(sic) world, an effortful world, a humorless world, a world without privacy or independence."[140]

Placed in situations in which they cannot hope to succeed, where their dreams will never be fulfilled, where human effort is fruitless and useless, humans

---

[139] Maslow, A.H., The Farther Reaches of Human Nature, pg. 141
[140] ibid., pp. 141-142

will fall down the same development ladder that they previously moved up on. "It is my impression that most people move away from B-Values under hard or bad environmental conditions that threaten the D-need gratifications."[141] This loss of personal well-being will also reflect negatively upon society in general. In countries and societies in which hopelessness as well as other negative societal characteristics exist, healthcare costs increase, the number of hospital stays rises, crime flourishes, and the number of suicides increases.

Additionally, Dr. Maslow also provided clinically observed examples of the effects on human beings in societies in which the B-Values and Basic Human Needs were thwarted: "In those countries in which...official theories were profoundly contradicted by obvious facts, at least some people responded with generalized cynicism, mistrust of all values, suspicion even of the obvious, a profound disruption of ordinary interpersonal relationships, hopelessness, loss of morale, etc.."[142]

The goal of society must be to provide the basic necessary framework for life for its members. This framework cannot logistically be provided for each member of society individually. Rather, an environment must be created in which it is possible for each member to expand and explore his or her own capabilities, while providing the necessary societal constraints to insure the common good and protect the right of other individuals to pursue their per-

---

[141] Maslow, A.H., The Farther Reaches of Human Nature, pg. 140
[142] Maslow, A.H., Motivation and Personality, pg. 96

sonal fulfillment. "One can set up social institutions which will guarantee that individuals will be at each other's throats; or one can set up social institutions which will encourage individuals to be synergic with each other. That is, one can set up social conditions so that one person's advantage would be to another person's advantage rather than the other person's disadvantage."[143]

Having transformed or set up social conditions in such a way as to facilitate a person's self-actualization, a society will reap multiple benefits. These will include a reduction in crime, a reduction in health care costs, a reduction in the rate of suicides. Looking at the situation from a perspective of gains achieved, a society will have provided the necessary framework so that the most creative members of society are able to do what they do best – to create. Facilitating creativity will always lead to prosperity.

This is a classic entreaty for a world similar to that described in Henderson's Win-Win World. It also describes ideals supported by Inglehart's Postmodernists, which are very similar to the values of Florida's Creative Class. Once again we have the reciprocal situation described previously. It is possible to set up social situations which are conducive to fostering the development of level five(M) individuals in society. On the other hand, it is usually the level five(M) individuals in society who are interested in changing their environments in this way. The one is in symbiosis with the other and, as the one flourishes, so does the other.

---

[143] Maslow, A.H., Eupsychian Management: A
    Journal, pp. 88-107

3.5 Clare W. Graves and The Levels of Human Existence

"A scientific truth does not triumph by convincing its opponents and making them see the light, but rather because its opponents eventually die and a new generation grows up that is familiar with it." Max Planck

Around the time that Abraham Maslow was perfecting his theory of "The Hierarchy of Needs" (1952-1959), a fellow researcher and professor of psychology at Union College in Schenectady, N.Y., Dr. Clare W. Graves, had grown tired of teaching the many differing views of human needs and psychological development offered by psychologists throughout the ages. He had also grown tired of playing referee in the endless debate about which one of them provided *the* answer.

Having become so frustrated that he wanted to quit his job entirely, he then devised a system of experiments which allowed him to continue teaching while at the same time conducting trials to determine the values of students taking part in his classes. The students ranged in age from 18 to 64. His goal was to provide the ultimate answer to the question of human psychological structure and to halt the constant debate between the differing treatment options and philosophies offered to psychologists.

Whereas Maslow developed his theory primarily upon observations, Graves began his research, not with a theory, but entirely without a theory. He simply wanted to allow the data of his study to provide the theory. Initially, the research began by

167

taking primary level students of psychology and forbidding them to read any literature on psychological theory whatsoever. In this way he wanted to obtain an unbiased answer to his primary question. This question was: "What is your own personal conception of what a healthy personality is?"[144]

After collecting the initial responses of each student he then subjected these students to both peer pressure and authoritative pressure to see how and if they would defend their answers. During the last segment of the course he once again asked the students to reply to the posed question and their rejoinders gave an accurate account of how these students responded to those external pressures.

What followed was a period of reflection to decide if these various responses could be categorized into different types. To this end, Graves asked various colleagues over a period of years to determine if there was any organizing principle which could be used to systematize the answers received. The results of the analysis were astonishing.

What these judges determined was that in 60% of the cases two major classifications of categories of psychological health could be determined, these were: "a.) health is denying/sacrificing the self; or b.) health is expressing the self"[145]. Following further research, Graves determined that these two major categories had a number of sub-categories each, and that these categories did not represent, as originally

---

[144] Graves, Clare W., Levels of Human Existence,
   Santa Barbara: ECLET Publishing, 2002, pg. 13
[145] ibid., pg. 17

thought, psychological health, instead, the categories represented personality systems.

So his conclusion was that the goal of previous psychological theory and practice; that is, to produce a certain type of psychological profile in a person, was a mistake because: "as soon as we produce a person who functions well in one system, the last thing he wants to be is that kind of a human being any longer. It bores the hell out of him. He wants to start behaving in some other new and different way."[146]

This process of reflection led to the conclusion that psychological health was not a static thing but a dynamic process. "Psychological health is a process;...it is a hierarchical process;...it is an open ended hierarchical process."[147] So Graves reached a similar conclusion to Maslow, however, his conclusion was based upon clinical research.

Having classified the personality categories, the next step in the process was to test the subjects according to various psychological tests in order to determine each classification's characteristics. Among the tests used within the groups were:

1. Group results on standardized tests
2. How subjects with similar conceptions organized to solve problems
3. How subjects with similar conceptions interacted with each other

---

[146] Graves, Clare W., Levels of Human Existence,
   Santa Barbara: ECLET Publishing, 2002, pg. 57
[147] ibid., pg. 28

4. How subjects with similar conceptions worked toward the solutions of the problems
5. How long, on average, it took each group to find answers
6. How many solutions each group found
7. Quality of answers found by groups (All groups found good answers but they differed as to how they found the answers and the number of answers that they found)
8. Average time of finding solutions (quantitative answers)[148]

After having subjected the groups to various tests, conclusions were drawn with respect to the test results. The results themselves were very interesting. One of the most important test results concerned the group categorized by Dr. Graves as G-T or the *"express self but not at the expense of others group"*. Here he discovered that "the *express self but not at the expense of others* (group) found more solutions (to the posed problems) than all other (groups) put together"[149]. This is a significant finding because, as Graves himself recognized, "this *express self but not at the expense of others* (group) is very much like Maslow's self-actualizing man and Rogers' fully functioning person and those descriptions."[150] Once again, whereas Maslow determined the character-

---

[148] Graves, Clare W., Levels of Human Existence, Santa Barbara: ECLET Publishing, 2002, pg. 31
[149] ibid.
[150] ibid., pp. 25-26

istics of his "healthy human being" on the basis of observations, Graves reached similar conclusions based upon scientific research.

However, in order to exclude the possible argumentation that the differing test results were the result of differing levels of intelligence, Graves also researched into the groups' IQ. After examining the gathered results, Graves determined that "there was no essential difference in intelligence ranking among the people."[151] So the differing amounts and quality of solutions produced by the *"express self but not at the expense of others"* group was not the result of a difference in intelligence level. Instead, certain inherent traits or values held by this group allowed them to produce far more creatively that their counterparts in the other personality categories. This point will be touched upon later.

Finally, as a result of the research, Graves concluded that: "my research suggests that eight major value systems have emerged to date. They are the reactive, the traditionalistic, the exploitive, the sacrificial, the materialistic, the sociocratic, the existential and the experiential value systems."[152] These value systems, or personality categories, correspond in great part to Maslow's "Hierarchy of Human Needs". In addition to the fact that Graves determined that the psychological development of humans is a systematic process, he also allowed for the possibility that additional value systems could

---

[151] Graves, Clare W., Levels of Human Existence,
    Santa Barbara: ECLET Publishing, 2002, pg. 32
[152] ibid., pg. 144

develop as human beings further developed as a species.

The first group designated by Graves was the reactive group. "It is a value system...where man is motivated only by his imperative needs. Since he is so motivated, since he lives by his built-in reflexological equipment, since he learns by imprinting and since he lacks awareness of himself as a separate and distinct being and has no consciousness of self, his values at this level are purely reactive in character...In a moral sense this is an amoral system. There is no should or ought in behavior because man, when centralized at this level does not operate cognitively. He only reacts. He does not think or judge or believe."[153] This first level corresponds identically to Maslow's first level in his "Hierarchy of Needs".

The second personality system classified by Graves was the traditionalistic system. In this system the person subjugates himself to the rules and values of his society in order to ensure the survival of the group. His personal needs are secondary. What is important is the respect of the status quo. "The prime end value at the second level is safety and the prime means value is tradition...Thus, man's theme for existence at this level is 'one shall live according to the ways of one's elders', and his values are consonant with this existential theme."[154] This system corresponds loosely to the second level of Maslow's hierarchy. However, certain aspects of his

---

[153] Graves, Clare W., Levels of Human Existence,
Santa Barbara: ECLET Publishing, 2002, pp. 144-145
[154] ibid., pg. 146

second level of needs are also found in Grave's third system. Therefore these two systems can be viewed as subcategories of the second Maslovian level.

At the third level, the exploitive level, "the energy previously devoted to finding ways to satisfy man's physiological needs and to the maintenance of tribal ways now released, awakens him to the recognition that he is a separate and distinct being...Now, aware of himself as an individual being, now aware of the need to foster his individual survival...Man begins to adjust the environment to his needs and seeks a primordial form of existence which he can control for his personal survival, not just one of automatic re-activity...Driven by the need to maintain his existence, each manipulates his world and egocentrically interprets the reward or punishment feedback as fostering or not fostering his own survival...He who wins has a right to loot the world to his own ends. Those who lose have a right only to the scraps he will toss their way. Might is right. The power ethic prevails."[155]

The third level personality, therefore, seeks to insure a personal survival through the control of others. However, the ultimate goal is, as it is in level two, the achievement of security. Both level two and three serve to provide security, the designated second Maslovian level. The second Graves level concentrates on achieving security for the group and the third level on the security of the individual, even to the detriment of the others. Therefore they can be

---

[155] Graves, Clare W., Levels of Human Existence,
Santa Barbara: ECLET Publishing, 2002, pg. 147

viewed as two sub-categories of the same aspect of security.

The next Graves level, the sacrificial level, corresponds to the Maslovian level for belonging and love. Here it was found that certain aspects of the belonging and love level are also found in Graves' level six personality category. However, a difference exists between the two groups as to how this love is expressed and also, primarily, what the goal of this expression of belongingness should achieve. "At the fourth level man does not propitiate his spirits for removal of threat to his immediate existence. Rather he is on a quest for everlasting peace. Here man's search for his Nirvana peaks in those absolutistic, sacrificial values which, if followed, will assure him that he will achieve the end which he values most, the end that is known as salvation...At this level man accepts his position and his role in life. Inequality is a fact of life. He believes the task of living is to strive for perfection in his assigned role...What one wants, or desires is not important. What is important is that he disciplines himself to the prescription of his world. Thus, the prime value of fourth level man is self-sacrifice...The leader values the life that enables him, if necessary, to sacrifice his self in the protection of the led. The led values sacrificing self in support of the leader."[156]

This means that partnerships, marriages or entries into group systems which take place within this level are expressions of sacrifice. An individual sacrifices certain aspects or all aspects of his own person-

---

[156] Graves, Clare W., Levels of Human Existence,
    Santa Barbara: ECLET Publishing, 2002, pg. 149

ality in order to participate within a group environment. The phenomenon of the entry into a cult can also be explained as an aspect of this personality system or developmental level.

The two Graves levels which follow the sacrificial values level can also be explained as corresponding to the Maslovian level of respect and self-esteem. Here, once again, as in the second Maslovian level, the two Graves levels offer specific aspects of the same phenomenon and can therefore be viewed as sub-groups of the same level. According to Maslow, a human being who is at this level of development seeks the respect of his peers. Additionally, self-esteem as a reflection of who one is and what one has accomplished is a desired and sought after characteristic. This desire for respect and self-esteem has two forms of expression within Graves' classifications.

The fifth level person(G), the person with materialistic values, seeks the respect of others primarily through visible and physical means. This is the level at which man seeks to acquire luxury goods as a status symbol, seeks to belong to the correct groups, seeks to achieve honors in the realm of sporting competitions, etc.

"At the fifth level...the theme for existence is 'express self in a way that rationality says is good for me now, but carefully, calculatedly so as not to bring down the wrath of others upon me.' Fifth level materialistic values...are values of accomplishing and getting, having and possessing...he values equality of opportunity and the mechanistic, measuring, quantitative approach to problems, including man. He values gamesmanship, competition, the entrepreneurial attitude, efficiency, work simplification, the calculated risk, scientific scheming and manipulation. But these fifth level, self-centered values are not (the)...egocentric values of the third level system...Fifth level values improve immeasurably man's conditions for existence...But to the fourth level man they are akin to sin, to the sixth they are the crass materialism of 'The Status Seeker'."[157] The physical signs of success are the tools used to acquire the respect of others. They may also help the person to achieve some level of self-esteem. However, the majority of self-esteem is gained when the person reaches level six in Graves.

The level of sociocratic values, the sixth values level, is a level at which the respect of others and self esteem is also sought. However, the method of achieving these aspects contrasts from the fifth level. In the fifth level respect and esteem are sought by means of possessing. The possession of material things is thought to bring the desired effect. But, "...at the sixth level it is the feelings of man, rather than the hidden secrets of the physical universe, which draw his attention. Consumer goodwill takes precedence over free enterprise, cooperation stands out as more valued that competition and social approval is valued over individual fame. Consumption and warm social intercourse are more valued at this level than are production and cold, calculation self interest. Here man values commonality over differential classification. The other aspect is his return to religiousness which again he values as he

[157] Graves, Clare W., Levels of Human Existence,
    Santa Barbara: ECLET Publishing, 2002, pp. 151-152

did in the previous adjustive systems...It is the spiritual attitude, the tender touch which he reveres."[158]

At this level interpersonal relationships become paramount. Both private relationships as well as professional relationships, bring the desired respect of others. Here, it is human contact, and not physical things which bring about the sought-after self-esteem. In some respects this level corresponds to level four, however, it differs in certain key aspects. In level four the person sacrifices his personal desires in order to belong. In level six the relationships are used as a means to support and strengthen the self.

The sixth level is the last of the subsistence levels. The subsistence levels are the levels of human development where the emphasis is on survival and "I". After having gone through the initial six levels of psychological development, the person no longer has to concentrate upon surviving; the person can now turn his thoughts to other, more important aspects of life. He has now reached the second major step in his personal development: the jump from the subsistence levels to the being levels of development.

Graves discovered that the seventh level of development contrasted sharply in many respects to the first six categories. So much so, that it was necessary to create a split between the two different category types. This division was underscored by the results of the tests applied to the different groups. "The thing that...stopped me cold for awhile...was this: the 'express self but not at the expense of others

---

[158] Graves, Clare W., Levels of Human Existence, Santa Barbara: ECLET Publishing, 2002, pp. 152-153

(group)' found more solutions than all the others put together. The average period of time required to arrive at a solution was much shorter than the other groups. The quality of the solutions arrived at was better than the other groups. This system was very, very different – incredibly different."[159] The idea that the differences in test results were the result of differences in levels of intelligence was also tested. "...We used any method at our disposal and we couldn't find any differences. And yet these people in this system simply came up with more answers, better answers in less time ...When a human being starts to think in this manner, that thinking evidences a personality re-organization that is almost unbelievable in character and it must be represented in this conceptualization."[160]

Graves then theorized as to why this overwhelming difference in test results occurred. "...What I find explains best to me the reason that the people in the G-T level behave so much better quantitatively and qualitatively, time-wise, etc., is this—they simply are not afraid. They are not afraid of not finding food (A-N). They are not afraid that they're not going to have shelter (B-O). They are not afraid of predatory man (C-P). They are not afraid of God (D-Q). They are not afraid of not having status or not making it on their own in this world (E-R). They are not afraid of social rejection (F-S)."[161]

---

[159] Graves, Clare W., Levels of Human Existence,
   Santa Barbara: ECLET Publishing, 2002, pg. 47
[160] ibid.
[161] ibid., pg. 67

The fulfillment of the lower human needs (Maslow) allowed the people in Graves' G-T level group to concentrate on higher goals. A constant fear for survival was solved through the societal aspects which gave these people the needed security with respect to subsistence. This allowed them to become creative individuals and to express their creativity. This idea corresponds identically to the theory of the "self-actualizing" human of Maslow and corre-

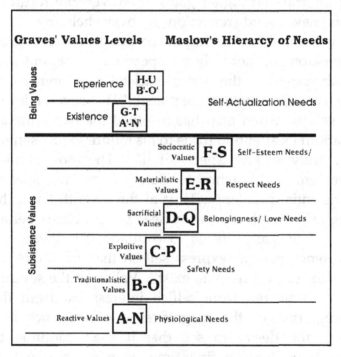

Figure 14. Clare W. Graves' Values Levels vs. Maslow's Hierarchy of Needs
Source: Author

sponds to the idea of the rise in number of independent problem-solvers in our developed societies today.

"The seventh level of existence develops from the resolution of man's animalistic problems...now

179

...after being hobbled by the more narrow animal-like needs...*suddenly* human cognition is free. Now with his energies free for cognitive activation, man focuses upon his self and his world. The picture revealed is not pleasant. Illuminated in devastating detail is man's failure to be what he might be and his misuse of his world."[162]

Once having been freed of the need to struggle for survival on a daily basis, man is now able to concentrate on higher goals. However, the result of this new-found reflection is overwhelming. Man now is capable of seeing the cost of his psychological development; not only in a personal sense, but also with respect to the cost of societal development on the ecological state of the planet. "The (seventh level) develops when man has resolved the basic human fears...His attention turns to his failure to focus upon the truly salient aspects of life...The most serious problem of existence to date is now his species 'existential problem'...Thus at the seventh level, the cognitive level, man truly sees the problems before him if life, any life, is to continue. His theme for existence is now 'express self so that all others, all beings, can continue to exist'...Values at the seventh level come not from selfish interest but from the recognition of the magnificence of existence and from the desire to see that it shall continue to be...Now, for the first time, man is able to face existence in all its dimensions, both those which seem to be known and those which are unexplained,

---

[162] Graves, Clare W., Levels of Human Existence,
   Santa Barbara: ECLET Publishing, 2002, pp. 153-154

even to the point of valuing inconsistencies, oppositions and flat contradictions."[163]

This trend is also documented in the scientific results of research conducted by Dr. Ronald Inglehart. The advancement towards ecological themes and a growing respect for the environment is part of this movement from subsistence levels to being levels (Graves) or the movement from the lower human needs levels to the level of self-actualization (Maslow). Another sign of this progression is the growing concern about the quality of food products, the popularity of biologically produced food and an interest in eliminating world hunger.

Additionally, Graves examined the person with level seven values with respect to his fellow human beings and discovered that: "he values the genuine acceptance of human nature as it is and shuns artificiality and preference for what it should be. He values all human appetites but is not a compulsive slave to any of them. He values spontaneity and simplicity and ethics that 'make sense' —but not conventionality...The activity is more important than any acclaim that may result. He values solving problems more than fulfilling selfish desires and what must be done rather than that which he desires to do. Universality is valued over provinciality and broadness of view is preferred to pettiness. He values the long run of time, even beyond his life...A few deep relationships mean more to him than broad acceptance by other men. Faith is more important than religion and viable ends determine more his

[163] Graves, Clare W., Levels of Human Existence, Santa Barbara: ECLET Publishing, 2002, pp. 154-155

behavior than do the means to the ends. Above all else he values democracy in the very deepest sense...He values pluralism. He values that which will enable all animals, all plants and things to be, and all mankind to become. His ethics are based on the best possible evidence as to what will benefit all. Concern with the majority, the needy or the desiring is not enough. He values that which will bring good to him and all the universe."[164] These are, once again, values which are squarely within the range of values of the self-actualized person as reported by Maslow. One can also recognize the echo of values of the Creative Class as presented by Richard Florida and the Postmodernist societal members studied by Ronald Inglehart.

However, just as each level of psychological development is seen as lacking by those who are currently within another developmental level, the seventh level or the level of the self-actualized human being has its detractors. "Oddly enough this value system is seen as decadent by many... because it values new ways, new structuring for life, not just the ways of one's elders. It values others as well as self, the enjoyment of this life over and above obeisance to authority, others having 'just as much as me', and it values all and self, not just the selected few."[165]

This means that this value level poses a serious threat to all of the others who favor the status quo or the survival of few to the detriment of the others.

---

[164] Graves, Clare W., Levels of Human Existence,
    Santa Barbara: ECLET Publishing, 2002, pp. 155-156
[165] ibid., pg. 156

182

Additionally, Graves commented that the G-T level is actually the repetition of the first level of human existence, albeit at a higher level. Now, instead of focusing on the preservation of himself, the human begins to focus on the preservation of life in general and of his species (human beings) in particular. In this manner Graves argued that the being levels are therefore a repetition of the lower six levels at a higher state of consciousness. This idea was also carried forward within the next psychological level, the eighth level.

At the time of his research, Graves only was able to touch upon the next value level, which had only begun to emerge at the time of his research. "The eighth level values are called the experientialistic values. Here man values those 'vast realms of consciousness still undreamed of, vast ranges of experience like the humming of unseen harps we know nothing of within us.'[166] He values wonder, awe, reverence, humility, fusion, integration, unity, simplicity, the poetic perception, enlarging consciousness, the ineffable experience (Maslow, 1962)."[167] Using commentary from Maslow, Graves explained his research results and concluded that this idea was another form of repetition of the idea of security and traditionalistic values.

Another explanation might be that, as in the levels two and four of Maslow, the level five also has two forms of expression within Graves' values

[166] de Sola Pinto, Vivian; Roberts, Warren (eds.),
    The complete Poems of D.H. Lawrence
    (Volumes I & II)., New York: The Viking Press, 1964
[167] Graves, Clare W., Levels of Human Existence,
    Santa Barbara: ECLET Publishing, 2002, pg. 156

system. "Now, let's look at what Maslow said. You should know that Maslow came around to my point of view. If you look at some of his later writing you will see that he accepted both the cyclic idea that there are more than one kind of expressive system and more than one kind of belonging system, and that the system is open ended...We finally, after fighting this over for eight or more years, came to a final agreement along this line."[168]

Currently, the world is in the middle of a transition period. The research of Inglehart showed that the modern world is fast adopting the values of a postmodern world. Developed nations are beginning to internalize values which are in direct contrast to the dominant economic model of Capitalism. This has resulted in the rise in importance of a new type of person. Called by many different names, these people exhibit characteristics and life skills desperately needed in these troubled times.

The scientists Maslow and Graves both set out to study these people, though they each chose to pursue this goal in differing manners. Both scientists recognized that a fundamental shift in thinking processes led to an explosion in creativity and skill. When examined together, the theoretical basis of Maslow and the scientific research of Graves offer a foundation for predicting the future of societies on this planet—a future which will begin when the majority of people in power positions are level five, self-actualizing people.

---

[168] Graves, Clare W., Levels of Human Existence,
   Santa Barbara: ECLET Publishing, 2002, pg. 52

3.6 Inclusivism™—Society Moves to the Next Level

"Apparently the organism is most unified in its integration when it is successfully facing either a great joy of creative moment or else a major problem or a threat or emergency. But when the threat is overwhelming or when the organism is too weak or helpless to manage it, it tends to disintegrate. On the whole when life is easy and successful, the organism can simultaneously do many things and turn in many directions."[169] Abraham Maslow

The primary motivational force in a human being is the desire to fulfill his innermost intrinsic needs. These needs range from the lowest needs of daily sustenance to the highest needs of self-fulfillment or self-actualization. Societies can either create an environment in which its members can achieve their highest potential or an environment in which these needs are constantly thwarted, leading ultimately to their physical and mental deterioration.

The goal of a society must then be to create conditions which allow its members to fulfill their needs. "I have already pointed out that one usable operational meaning of the 'good society' is the degree to which it offers all its members the basic need satisfactions and the possibilities of self-actualization and human fulfillment. To this phrasing can be added the proposition 'the good society' (by contrast with the poor society) exemplifies, values,

---

[169] Maslow, A.H., Motivation and Personality, pg. 75

strives for, (and) makes possible the achievement of the B-Values."[170]

The benefit to a society which provides these conditions is, at the lowest level, its survival. At the higher level, however, a society which provides this framework can hope to achieve and hold economic, social and developmental superiority over other societies which do not. "To come back to my title (The Creative Attitude), what I'm talking about is the job of trying to make ourselves over into people who don't need to staticize (sic) the world, who don't need to freeze it to make it stable,...who are able confidently to face tomorrow not knowing what's going to come, not knowing what will happen, with confidence enough in ourselves that we will be able to improvise in that situation which has never existed before. This means a new type of human being. Heraclitian, you might call him. The society which can turn out such people will survive; the societies that cannot turn out such people will die."[171]

The theories and subsequent clinical observations of Dr. Abraham Maslow provide a useful tool for creating a methodology for the improvement of the conditions of society in general. By applying his Basic Human Needs theory, it very quickly becomes apparent which role a society or city needs to play in order to provide a framework in which its members can develop themselves and their potentials to the fullest. Furthermore, a society which successfully provides this framework insures not

---

[170] Maslow, A.H., The Farther Reaches of Human
    Nature, pg. 142

[171] ibid., pg. 59

only its own survival, but also the improvement of the physical and mental health of its members. In an age in which the skyrocketing costs of healthcare have created problems for all developed nations, the benefits of applying this methodology are all too obvious.

Even in his day, Graves recognized that developed societal systems were in a state of fluctuation. This process was in the beginning stages during his experiments and has continued at a steady rate until today. "Today seventh level man, with his mind open for cognitive roaming, is developing the coming mode of life...Western man at this moment in history is approaching his great divide, the landmark between *subsistence level systems* and *being level systems*."[172] This means that a great change in values is under way and that this change in value systems offers great potential for human kind "...a sudden and almost unbelievable change in human behavior takes place when the individual begins to believe that psychological health should be both expressive of self and taking care of the other human being at the same time."[173]

Having recognized that success in life no longer has to be at the expense of others, the developed world will then be in a position to offer creative solutions which benefit all and not just a few. With the growing number of societal members who hold these values, the traditionalist values will be rejected and the result will be a better standard of living for

---

[172] Graves, Clare W., Levels of Human Existence, Santa Barbara: ECLET Publishing, 2002, pg. 154
[173] ibid., pg. 47

all on the planet. Danger inherent in this transition, however, lies in form of resistance against this metamorphosis from societies which are squarely within the subsistence levels of development.

This will especially be the case in societies which are currently at level two and three (Graves) and the safety level (Maslow). Here, the changes in the existing value systems will be construed as a threat to personal and societal security and could result in violent resistance to this new form of social structure and the new value system. This is because the value system might be viewed as being imposed upon the less developed nations by the more developed nations.

In cases where the citizens are at a higher level of development than their leaders, entrenchment of the ruling elite could manifest as violence against their own people. Rulers might bunker themselves into their bulkheads and resist any attempts at removal. Additionally, leaders might seek to arrest protesters and hinder all forms of protest against the entrenched political establishment, even to the point of killing those protesters.

Currently the world is experiencing the physical, social and economic manifestation of the movement of the developed world from the subsistence needs to the being needs. The signs of this transformation are everywhere: the increase in awareness of human responsibility for the state of the natural world; the increase in awareness of the responsibility of the developed world for the state of the developing world; the increase of an acute awareness of the necessity for high-quality food products and methods of preparation (Maslow's level one needs at a higher state of consciousness).

The current widespread anger of the mass of the citizens (level five) with the excessive greed and egotism exhibited by certain business sectors of society (level four), which caused the current worldwide economic crisis, is probably the most obvious of these manifestations. Assisted in their development through international internet social and informational platforms, the majority of the citizens in the developed world has already moved beyond level four thinking into level five thinking. Unfortunately, the vast majority of major corporations and their board members as well as the overwhelming majority of political leaders are still squarely within level four thinking. This causes political dissatisfaction and unrest.

It would be extremely simplistic to suggest that this alteration in thinking is simply a generational change, although the number of level five thinkers *is* higher among younger members of society. Instead what has happened is that the general security, freedom and provision of the basic essentials, which has occurred within the developed world during the last sixty or so years, has provided the framework for the further psychological development of the greater part of the citizenry. The majority of citizens has moved beyond spending the bulk of their time thinking about existential needs and has now moved onto thinking about being needs.

According to the findings of Maslow and Graves and the description of the characteristics of these level five thinkers, what awaits us now should be one of the most prosperous and just time periods in the history of mankind. Level five thinkers have the best chance of bringing humanity out of the mess in which it finds itself. Level five thinkers are capable of producing more and better solutions to problems than all other levels combined. Level five thinkers are not interested in the success of the few to the detriment of the many; instead, level five thinkers want the success of the many **and the few** (or one).

Unfortunately, there is just one potential hindrance to this scenario. Level four thinkers, who currently hold the majority of power and economic power positions throughout the developed world, are not going to give up their positions without a fight. When asked to step down from their positions, they deny wrong-doing, take up court fights, and refuse to acknowledge that it is time to go. When ordered to pay back extravagant bonuses paid out of taxpayer pockets, they refuse. When accused of and charged with racketeering, tax evasion and other financial crimes, they try to hide the illegally gotten gains.

Already there are very concrete examples of this transition happening throughout the world. The Arab Spring with the overthrow of the long-standing governments of Tunesia and Egypt demonstrated the power of level five thinking when brought against old, entrenched level three/four dictatorships and family dynasties.

The events unfolding in Libya are probably the most understandable example of the violent form of this transition process. In the west of the country, Muammar Gaddafi and his power entourage have bunkered themselves in the capital. Paid mercenaries and militia are attacking and bombing cities filled with unarmed civilians in an effort to stem rebel advancements. The armed rebels are retaliating, but are hopelessly under-equipped.

In the east of the country a new society is being built. Young, well-educated members of the rebellion are building a society based upon innovation and the inclusion of all members of society. Here, free television and radio stations are being organized to disseminate vital information to the citizenry. New businesses are being formed and governmental structures are being constructed based upon inclusive principles. In contrast, the state-run television is broadcasting the same disinformation and propaganda that it always had.

The developed world is currently standing at the precipice of a great divide. The most awesome potential awaits on the other side of this divide. Given access to positions of influence throughout society, level five thinkers will begin to implement changes to the entire societal structure. Systems will be implemented that benefit the greatest majority of inhabitants on the planet. These systems will not just benefit the few, but also the many. Thus the new societal form of Inclusivism™ will be born. It is possible to make such sweeping statements, if one examines the characteristics and values of these level five thinkers, these independent problem-solvers, these postmodern members of society, and these Creative Class citizens. The values that a person holds and the person's characteristics provide the foundation for the actions of that person. If one knows the character traits and values of an individual, one can, with great certainty, predict how this individual will react and act in different situations.

One should not fear a world in which the majority of power holders are level five thinkers, unless one is still firmly within the self-absorption of the other thinking levels. Faced with the current problems, individuals who have reached the being levels are not likely to fall back down to the lower levels because the change in psychological condition and thought processes between the fourth and fifth thinking levels is so profound and so fundamental. The lower thinking levels, however, do tend to move backwards when confronted with outside adversity.

The choice lies in the hands of humanity—to move forwards or backwards. "In our world of past and present there are societies and people at all levels, and societies and peoples whose levels are mixed...All men do not progress and some societies may wither and die. Man may never cross his great divide but on the other hand, he may. ...so the problem of ethical and moral decline lies, this theory says, not so much in the breakdown and discard of 'the old' as in the retention of existentially inappropriate values during a period of profound transformation in human existence."[174]

---

[174] Graves, Clare W., Levels of Human Existence,
Santa Barbara: ECLET Publishing, 2002, pg. 157

Chapter Four
WHAT HAPPENS NEXT?

Life after the Transformation

"We frail humans are at one time capable of the greatest good and, at the same time, capable of the greatest evil. Change will only come about when each of us takes up the daily struggle ourselves to be more forgiving, compassionate, loving, and above all joyful in the knowledge that, by some miracle of grace, we can change as those around us can change too." Mairead Maguire

Birth Pains

There have been numerous signs of the beginning of the social revolution coming upon us. The first major indication was the fall of the Berlin Wall and the reunification of Germany followed by the overthrow of the Communist led Eastern Block countries and the fall of the Iron Curtain. Since then, the signals have been coming with ever greater frequency and ever greater intensity.

The ousting of the Tunisian president (of 23 years); the overthrow of the entire Egyptian government (and a dictator of 29 years); the growing unrest in Algeria, Yemen, Bahrain, Libya, Iran and other nations in the Middle East; the Tea Party movement in the United States; mass demonstrations in virtually every developed country; marches for more environmental responsibility; and a shift of power back to the people are all indications of the metamorphosis of a society driven by Capitalism to one led by the ideology of Inclusivism™. However, the resistance to the change is also evident.

Environmental disasters caused by gross corporate mismanagement (an indication of level four thinking gone mad); the extension of the operational period for outdated and potentially dangerous nuclear power plants against the will of the majority of citizens; a widespread weakness and laxity of political figures to grasp the initiative and instigate any type of necessary long-term structural change; the extreme profit orientation (greed) of the international banking system—even to the detriment of worldwide financial stability; are all indications of the resistance of the status quo to the new values and ideals of the citizenry.

Looking into the future one can predict that this general state of affairs will continue for some time to come, unless catastrophic events force a more expedient transformation. This transitional period is necessary, as the older generation, entrenched in the level three and four thinking of their forefathers, needs to lose hold of the economic and political power positions within society. Additionally, more economic uncertainties and periods of upheaval can be anticipated as the financial system adjusts to the new realities. The threat of terrorism will continue as a result of the feeling of helplessness against these changes experienced by level three Maslovian societies.

In order to combat this imminent change, level four societies and institutions will begin a course of massive encroachment upon the rights and freedoms of their citizens. Data will be gathered as a pre-emptive measure, but due to the close interdependency of level four politics and level four business, this data will not be held secret—it will be passed freely between these entities. Organizations fighting against the encroachment on civil liberties will experience pressure from both the political and financial sector. Ordinary and innocent citizens may be incarcerated as a result of the misuse of legally and illegally gathered data.

Politicians, caught in their old way of thinking and powerless to change anything within a system spinning its wheels will continue to propose laws and pass them. But these laws will do nothing to change the underlying structural problems of the system. Thus, the pressure within the old system will continue to build. Massive demonstrations and protests by the public at large will result.

On the other side of the issue, sovereign organizations representing the viewpoints and values of the independent problem solvers like: Wikileaks, Transparency International, Sea Shepherd, WWF, etc., will continue to gain in strength and support. In addition to this, a return to spiritual values will be heralded by a worldwide revival, as heightened spirituality is another trait of these people. This does not necessarily mean that existing church structures will experience a rebirth. Instead, the reawakening of spiritual values will take place primarily outside of existing church structures and systems.

These trends will intensify the pressure on the societal systems from both within and without. Faced with this mounting pressure, the current societal structures and systems will limp along until they finally collapse.

The Birth

Once the old system has collapsed and a general realization has spread that the old social methodologies are no longer valid and useful, the process of creating a new societal structure will begin. The increasing number and influence of the independent problems solvers will mean that they will begin to assume the positions of power and authority vacated by the old leaders. An exchange of values will accompany the transition of power.

These people, called "healthy" or "self-actualized" by Maslow, will bring with them a whole new set of ideals and values which they will then apply to the problems facing society. A list of the characteristics of these people can be found on page 156 of this work and a list of their values on page 158. Based upon these traits and ideals, a scenario of the new social order can be created.

Having assumed positions of power and taken leadership roles in the new social structure, a period of assessment will follow. Self-actualizing people are problem-solvers. They have a superior perception of reality, which helps them to recognize the key source of problems. An accurate evaluation of the root of difficulties is essential as a first step towards solving them.

After the period of assessment, a period of reflection will follow. Healthy people are spiritual people. They have recognized that the current state of affairs in the world is a result of selfishness (in all of its forms) gone mad. As such, they also recognize that the solutions to the problems facing the world today are going to be created as a result of the careful evaluation of all facts related to the situation, followed by a period of introspection (prayer, meditation, reflection) through which the inspiration for the solution will come.

Self-actualizing people are private people. They are much more interested in finding *the* solution to a problem, applying the solution and then having the satisfaction of seeing the solution bring results, than they are in reaping accolades for having produced an answer. It is much more likely that a resolution produced by an independent problem solver be applied quietly and the ensuing changes evolve gradually, than it is for such a solution to be presented at a grand event with much fanfare (these are level four values). A healthy human being sees such events as both a waste of time and of money.

However, openness, honesty and democracy are also values held by these people. So the likelihood is that the solutions to the problems facing societies found through this process will be made public through new medias (internet, blogs, etc.). This is the most likely form of distribution, as it is the fastest, most expedient and most economical of all possibilities. And healthy human beings hate waste in all forms.

Once found, it is certain that the solution created will be one which will be the most advantageous. It will be a solution in which all benefit and none lose, a win-win-solution. This is the case because, as Graves discovered through his research, these people "found more solutions than all others (all other levels) put together...The quality of the solutions arrived at was better than the other groups."[175] The

---

[175] Graves, Clare W., Levels of Human Existence,

resolution will more than likely be one in which the greatest number of difficulties will be remedied by it. It will not solve one problem and create ten new ones in the process. Ultimately it will be the answer best suited to the difficulty, the actors, the environment and the circumstances because these problem-solvers are extremely creative people and, "what the superior man thinks is good, that is what is really good."[176]

Having then spent introspective time arriving at a solution to the problems facing the world, the independent problem solvers will then set about implementing these solutions to alter the state of affairs. As was previously discussed, Cultural Creatives are not exclusive to any one occupation. They can be found within any business, craft or income level. They have become independent problem solvers by means of a process of psychological and spiritual development. This means that anyone can become one and that they exist everywhere and in every level of society.

Healthy people are integrative. That means that they do not push themselves to the forefront, they do not seek praise for their work, they simply want to have an environment in which to explore their skills and abilities and develop themselves to the fullest. They would also like everyone else to have this same opportunity at self-progression.

Santa Barbara: ECLET Publishing, 202, pg. 47
[176] Maslow, A.H., The Farther Reaches of Human Nature, pg. 9

The World of Inclusivism™

Capitalism is about "me". Inclusivism™ is about "me-in-we". The world under a system of Inclusivism™ will be a far different world from the one in which we currently find ourselves. It will be a just world, as justice is a value highly prized by healthy human beings. However, this justice will not only be directed towards other people, it will also include the world in which we live. A justice, not for the people against the world and the environment, but a justice for the people *and* the environment.

Because of this, one of the first things that will begin to happen as a result of the coming social revolution is that the needs of the environment and nature will be integrated into all aspects of social life. The world will no longer be viewed as an always full pantry to be raided whenever the need arises. Instead, solutions to problems will be created which take into account the needs of the environment and incorporate them into the solution. The principles of Natural Capitalism and Sustainability will be evident here. Our raped world will begin to heal and with it, the people who live in it.

This will change the form of the built environment. Unchecked urban sprawl will be halted. Not solely for the sake of the environment, but also because endless expanses of suburban development are expensive to maintain. Inner city infrastructure will be renewed and empty lots will be converted to public green spaces, either parks or gardens. There will be increased investment in the public transportation systems as a means of improving the efficiency of transportation.

The integrative use of alternative energy sources will become the norm in new construction. Houses and buildings will become zero-energy, that is; they will cover 100% of their own energy needs through the production of energy in the structure. The integration of green space within buildings will also become standard. "Green lungs" will be incorporated as part of the overall design of the structure.

An increasing respect and appreciation for the environment will bring with it a regard for the preciousness of water as a natural resource. Buildings will begin to be built in such a way as to capture rainwater, filter it on site, use it, and then to recycle it multiple times to glean the greatest usage out of it. Once sent back into the system, the water will be cleaned and filtered to such an extent, that the reintroduced water will enter the environment cleaner than it was taken out.

The creation of electricity on site will encourage the production and use of electric vehicles. Beginning in Europe and then spreading to highly populated centers worldwide, these electric vehicles will become the rule as people realize the advantages of "filling-up" in the privacy and convenience of one's own home. The increased demand for electric vehicles will advance battery technology. Ultimately, the advance in battery technology will allow other vehicles to be converted to electric power. Trucks, airplanes and ships will eventually run on battery driven electricity.

It will be an egalitarian world. A world in which people will be accepted and valued regardless of which social level they are on or which job they do. Together with this, the hero worship of film stars, pop stars, rock stars and members of government/royalty will fade (these are level four values). In place of this, people will be valued for the things that they do within and for society. Their contribution will be valued, not their position. They will be appreciated for what they do and *that* they are, not who they are. Additionally, the people who consistently seek to exploit others and the environment for their personal gain will be held accountable for their actions, and recompense will be required. This value will permeate all aspects of society changing politics, business, entertainment and the financial system with it.

The creative spirit of every human being will be valued and respected. The educational system will change as a result. No longer will competition dominate the schools, but each student will be viewed as a potential bottomless source of new and better ideas. Students will be encouraged and supported in their development, allowed the freedom to explore skills, and helped along the path of self-actualization—regardless of their age or their social position. Through this, creative solutions to problems facing society will arise from the most unlikely places. Both children and retirees will present answers that will be both widely accepted and lauded.

Cleaning the environment will become a lucrative source of income. Raw materials will become so precious, that the reuse of discarded materials will become economically feasible. Landfills will be reopened and the long redundant waste removed, sorted, and recycled. The discarded plastic fragments soiling the oceans will be filtered out and recycled, thereby cleaning the waterways and restoring a natural resource.

Governments will discover that protecting and restoring natural environments is a profitable course of action. Through the designation of natural preservation areas, both on land and in the waterways and oceans, ecotourism will be encouraged. The conservation of ocean areas and resources will bring an increase in tourism revenue and former fishermen will be retrained as water rangers, protecting the natural resources they once decimated.

Businesses will begin to be run differently. Instead of a hierarchical system of top-down management (level four values), they will become more inclusive, integrating the ideas and suggestions of every member of the team into the equation. Salaries and bonuses will be decided upon collectively, effectively eradicating enviousness. A person's contribution to the enterprise will be prized, not their position.

The purpose of doing business will change. Businesses will provide goods and services as a means of solving problems and fulfilling needs. The profit motivation (level four values) will become secondary. In its place will come a greater sense of fulfillment, because the customer's needs are being met. Customer satisfaction and product quality will become priorities and the consumer will be included in the product development process. Having been integrated within the system, customer loyalty will be insured thereby fusing the product and the user into a symbiosis. A return of the pride of doing business and the pride of being associated with a business and a product will result.

Efficiency and customer orientation will cause the size of conglomerates to shrink. Large corporations are unwieldy and difficult to change. Because of the need to be flexible, these will break up into smaller, more elastic units. These units will be independent and autonomous small and medium-sized businesses bound together with others through cooperative efforts and creative synergy.

As a result, the stock markets with their anonymous trading of business potential and business speculation will change. With a plethora of small and medium-sized enterprises located within communities, investors will begin to take an active role in businesses in their neighborhoods. Investment will become local and personal instead of international and impersonal. Businesses will profit from this close contact with money people and the exchange of information and experience will be mutually beneficial.

The break-up of big corporations and the movement of investment capital to the local level will diminish the need for large international money exchanges and complex international banking structures. Banks will become local community institutions, where customers and their needs are known. Customers, that need financial help, will not only receive the funding, but will be supported through training and mentoring in order to guarantee the success of both the venture and the initiator. Local banks will be bound together through a system of cooperatives. This will ensure both the funding of larger projects, as well as the exchange of information and ideas. Once again, the focus will be on the fulfillment of customer needs, not the maximization of profits.

Politics and the political system will be radically changed. A top down political structure will no longer be tolerated. Instead, citizens will be included in every aspect of the governmental system. This is because they will be viewed as potential sources for solutions and not as the sources of the problems. Structural changes will take place within the bureaucracy. It will be streamlined and governmental employees will receive more autonomy in their decision-making. As a result things will begin to move much more quickly, backlogged requests being handled and taken care of expediently.

Coupled with this, public servants will again become that which they were meant to be— **SERVANTS**! Corruption will diminish, as the financial, personal and social cost of such behavior will increase so greatly, that the benefits of the conduct will be negligible. Many politicians will lose their seats of power due to the exposure of inappropriate behavior. With the reduction and eradication of corruption will come a veritable explosion in efficiency and publicly spent money will truly have the effect that it was intended to have.

The abandonment of hero worship (level four values) will bring with it a radical change in all forms of media. Entertainment will be found through education. Movies will not only tell stories, they will promote and instill values and pass helpful ideas on to the audience. Radio and television stations will begin to include shows within their programs which educate the audience on the latest developments and ideas, thereby spreading these solutions and creating a knowledge base upon which to build the next level of potential solutions. The recounting of true stories will take precedence over the narration of fiction.

Although the scenario presented here might seem very utopian and futuristic, the fact is that these changes have already started to take place. Banks, schools, businesses, government institutions and media enterprises already exist, which are run according to and incorporate the values of these independent problem solvers. Buildings and neighborhoods are being built, integrating the ideas of Sustainability and New Urbanism. Sources of alternative energy are being researched with a never before seen intensity. Electric driven motor vehicles have gone into large-scale production.

The current increase in indicative world events signify that a tipping point in world ideology is fast being approached. Once reached, the position and influence of institutions run on the basis of the obsolete system of Capitalism will begin to diminish until they either change, or become part of a collective past: a past which existed before the rise of Inclusivism™.

BIBLIOGRAPHY

Books

Adizes, Ichak, Managing Corporate Lifecycles, Paramus, NJ: Prentice Hall Press, 1999

Allaert, G.; Ventriss, C., The Impact of Information Technology on the Future of the City, Baltimore: Johns Hopkins University, Center of Metropolitan Planning and Research, 1984

Arendt, Randall G., Growing Greener: Putting Conservation into Plans and Ordinances, Washington, D.C.: Island Press, 1999

Barnett, Jonathan, The Elusive City: Five Centuries of Design, Ambition and Miscalculation, New York: Harper and Row, 1986.

Beck, Don Edward ; Cowan, Christopher ; Spiral Dynamics: Mastering Values, Leadership and Change, London: Blackwell Publishing Ltd., 1996, 2006

Bell, Daniel, The Coming of Post-Industrial Society, New York: Basic Books, 1973

Bianchini, Franco; Landry, Charles; The Creative City – Working Paper 3: Indicators of a Creative City, A Methodology for Assessing Urban Vitality and Viability, Bournes Green, UK: Comedia, 1994

Buchwald, Emilie, ed., Toward a Livable City, Milkweed Editions, 2003

Calthorpe, Peter; Van der Ryn, Sim; Sustainable Communities: A New Design Synthesis for Cities, Suburbs and Towns, California: Sierra Club Books, 1986

Congress for the New Urbanism, Charter of the New Urbanism: Region / Neighborhood, District, and Corridor / Block, Street, and Building, New York: McGraw-Hill Books, 1999

de Sola Pinto, Vivian; Roberts, Warren (eds.), The complete Poems of D.H. Lawrence (Volumes I & II)., New York: The Viking Press, 1964

Duany, Andres; Plater-Zyberk, Elizabeth; Towns and Town-Making Principles, New York: Rizzoli International Publications, Inc., 1991

Easterling, Keller; Mohney, David; Seaside: Making a Town in America, New York: Princeton Architectural Press, 1991

Florida, Richard, The Flight of the Creative Class, New York, 2005

Florida, Richard, The Rise of the Creative Class; and How It's Transforming Work, Leisure, Community and Everyday Life, New York: Basic Books, 2002

Fogel, Robert, The Fourth Great Awakening and the Future of Egalitarianism, Chicago: University of Chicago Press, 2000

Franke, Simon; Verhagen, Evert, Creativity and the City, Rotterdam: NAi Publishers, 2006

Frantz, Douglas; Collins, Catherine; Celebration, U.S.A.: Living in Disney's Brave New Town, New York: Henry Holt & Company, 1998

Friedman, Lawrence, The Horizontal Society, New Haven: Yale University Press, 1999

Gladwell, Malcolm, The Tipping Point – How Little Things Can Make a Big Difference, Boston: Little, Brown, and Company, 2002

Gladwell, Malcolm, Der Tipping Point – Wie Kleine Dinge Grosses Bewirken Können, Berlin: Berlin Verlag, 2002

Graves, Clare W., Levels of Human Existence (William R. Lee, editor), Santa Barbara: ECLET Publishing, 2002

Grogan, Paul S.; Proscio, Tony, Comeback Cities: A Blueprint for Urban Neighborhood Revival, Boulder, Oxford: Westview Press, 2000

Hawken, Paul; Lovins, Amory; Lovins, L. Hunter, Natural Capitalism, Boston: Little, Brown and Company, 1999

Henderson, Hazel, Building a Win-Win World – Life Beyond Global Economic Warfare, San Francisco: Berrett-Koehler Publishers, 1996

Hondrich, Karl Otto, Bedürfnisse – Stabilität und Wandel, Opladen: Westdeutscher Verlag GmbH, 1983

Horx, Matthias, Future Fitness – Wie Sie Ihre Zukunftskompetenz erhöhen. Ein Handbuch für Entscheider, Eichborn-Verlag, 2003

Inglehart, Ronald, Culture Shift in Advanced Industrial Society, Princeton: Princeton University Press, 1990

Inglehart, Ronald, Modernization and Post-modernization: Cultural, Economic and Political Change in Forty-Three Societies, Princeton: Princeton University Press, 1997

Inglehart, Ronald, The Silent Revolution: Changing Values and Political Styles in Advanced Industrial Society, Princeton: Princeton University Press, 1977

Jacobs, Jane, Cities and the Wealth of Nations, New York: Random House, 1984

Jacobs, Jane, The Death and Life of Great American Cities: The Failure of Town Planning, Harmondsworth, Middelsex: Peregrine / Penguin Books Ltd., 1984

Jacobs, Jane, The Economy of Cities, New York: Random House, 1969

Kahn, Bonnie Menes, Cosmopolitan Culture: The Gilt Edged Dream of a Tolerant City, New York: Simon and Schuster, 1987

Katz, Peter, The New Urbanism: Toward an Architecture of Community, New York: McGraw-Hill, 1994

Kaus, Mickey, The End of Equality, New York: Basic Books, 1992

Kemmis, Daniel, The Good City and The Good Life, New York: Houghton Mifflin, 1995.

Kennedy, Paul, The Rise and Fall of the Great Powers, New York: Vintage Books, 1989

Kennedy, Richard, London: World City Moving Into the 21st Century- A Research Project, London: HMSO, 1991

Kondratieff, Nikolai, The Long Wave Cycle, New York: Richardson & Snyder, 1984

Kruempelmann, Elizabeth, The Global Citizen: A Guide to Creating an International Life and Career, For Students Professionals, Retirees, and Families, Berkeley/ Toronto: Ten Speed Press, 2002

Landry, Charles, The Creative City – A Toolkit for Urban Innovators, London, Earthscan Publications, Ltd., 2000

Landry, Charles; Bianchini, Franco; Ebert, Ralph;
Gnad, Fritz; Kunzmann, Klaus R.; The Creative
City in Britain and Germany, London: Anglo-
German Foundation for the Study of Industrial
Society, 1996

Lennard, Suzanne H. Crowhurst, et al., Livable
Cities, Southampton, NY: Gondolier Press/Center
for Urban Well-Being, 1987

Lessinger, Jack, Penturbia: Where real estate will
boom after the crash of Suburbia, Seattle: Socio-
Economics, 1991

Marcuse, H., Eros and Civilization, Beacon Hill, 1955.

Makimoto, Tsugio; Manners, David, Digital Nomad,
West Sussex, England: John Wiley & Sons Ltd,
1997

Maslow, Abraham H., Eupsychian Management: A
Journal, Homewood, Ill.: Irwin Dorsey, 1965

Maslow, Abraham H., The Farther Reaches of
Human Nature, New York: The Viking Press,
1971

Maslow, Abraham H., Motivation and Personality,
New York, Evanston, and London: Harper &
Row, 1954

Maslow, Abraham H., Toward a Psychology of Being
– Second Edition, New York: Van Nostrand
Reinhold, 1968

Mellaart, James, Çatal Hüyük, A Neolithic Town in
Anatolia, London: Thames & Hudson, 1967

Mikunda, Christian, Der Verbotene Ort oder Die
inszenierte Verführung: Unwiderstehliches
Marketing durch strategische Dramaturgie,
Düsseldorf: ECON Verlag GmbH, 1996

Ministerium für Umwelt und Verkehr, Baden-Württemberg; Bayerischen Staatsministeriums für Landesentwicklung und Umweltfragen; Hessischen Ministeriums für Umwelt, Landwirtschaft und Forsten; Thüringer Ministerium für Landwirtschaft, Naturschutz und Umwelt, Leitfaden: Indikatoren im Rahmen einer Lokalen Agenda 21, Darmstadt: Druckhaus Darmstadt GmbH, November 2000

Mohney, David; Easterling, Keller, eds.; Seaside: Making a Town in America, New York: Princeton Architectural Press, 1991

OECD, Towards Sustainable Development: Indicators to Measure Progress, Rome Conference (December 15-17, 1999), Paris: OECD, 2000

Olson, Mancur; Landsberg, Hans H., ed.; The No-Growth Society, New York: W.W. Norton, 1973

Olson, Mancur, The Rise and Decline of Nations, New Haven, London:Yale University Press, 1982

Ray, Paul H.; Anderson, Sherry Ruth, The Cultural Creatives: How 50 Million People are Changing the World, New York: Harmony Books, 2000

Reiss, Steven, Ph.D., Who Am I? — The 16 Basic Desires That Motivate Our Behavior and Define Our Personality, New York: Jeremy P. Tarcher/ Putnam, 2000

Reynolds, Michael, Water from the Sky, Earthship Biotecture, www.earthship.org

Rifkin, Jeremy: The European Dream: How Europe's Vision of the Future Is Quietly Eclipsing the American Dream, New York: Jeremy P. Tarcher/Penguin, 2004

Schoon, Nicholas, The Chosen City, New York and Canada: Spon Press, 2001

Schulz, Gerhard, Die Erlebnisgesellschaft: Kultursoziologie der Gegenwart, Frankfurt/ Main, New York: Campus Verlag, 1993

Schumpeter, Joseph A., Business Cycles: A Theoretical, Historical and Statistical Analysis of the Capitalist Process, Vol. 1, New York and London: McGraw-Hill Book Company, Inc., 1939

Schumpeter, Joseph A., Capitalism, Socialism, and Democracy, New York and London: Harper & Brothers Publishers, 1942

Schumpeter, Joseph A., The Theory of Economic Development, New York: Oxford University Press, 1961

Smith, David M., Where the Grass is Greener – Geographical Perspectives on Inequality, London: Croom Helm, 1979

Soja, Edward W., Postmetropolis : Critical Studies of Cities and Regions, Oxford: Blackwell Publishers Ltd., 2000

Thomas, Bob, Walt Disney – An American Original, New York, 1976

United Nations, Department of International Economic and Social Affairs; Population Studies, No. 114: Trends in population Policy, New York: United Nations, 1989

United Nations, Education Program, 1993

United Nations, Department of Economic and Social Affairs, Population Division; World Economic and Social Survey 2002, New York: United Nations, 2002

Newspaper and Magazine Articles

Ahnström, L.: "The Turnaround Trend and the Economically Active Population of Seven Capital Regions in Western Europe", Norsk Geogr. Tidschrift, 40.2, pp. 55-64

Anonymous, Slack and Insufferable, The Australian, Australia's National Daily Newspaper, Jan. 22, 2004

Beckmann, Klaus J.: „Städtebaulicher Bericht „Nachhaltige Stadtentwicklung" – Eine neue Ära der Städtebaupolitik", Informationen zur Raumentwicklung, Heft 2/3 1996, pp. 117 – 135.

Beauregard, R.A: „Capital Restructuring and the new Built Environment of Global Cities. New York and Los Angeles", International Journal of Urban and Regional Research 15/1, 1991, pp. 90-105.

Beaverstock, J.V.; Smith, R.G.: „A Roster of World Cities", Cities, vol. 16/6, 1999, pp. 445-458.

Beaverstock, J.V.; Smith, R.G.; Taylor, P.: "World City Network: a New Metageography?", Annals of the Association of American Geographers 90, 2000, pp. 123-134.

Bookout, Lloyd W.: "Neotraditional Town Planning: Bucking Conventional Codes and Standards", Urban Land, June 1992, pp. 12-17.

Bookout, Lloyd W.: "Neotraditional Town Planning: Cars, Pedestrians, and Transit", Urban Land, February 1992, pp. 10-15.

Bookout, Lloyd W.: "Neotraditional Town Planning: A New Vision For the Suburbs?", Urban Land, January 1992, pp.20-26.

Bookout, Lloyd W.: "Neotraditional Town Planning: The Test of the Marketplace", Urban Land, June 1992, pp. 12-17.

Bookout, Lloyd W.: "Neotraditional Town Planning: Toward a Blending of Design Approaches", Urban Land, August 1992, pp. 14-19.

City of Fort Collins, Colorado, City Scape: A Portrait of Progress-2001 Report to the Community, pg. 3

Cuddy, Alison with Bruegmann, Robert, Chicago Public Radio, Eight Forty-Eight: "The Case for Success in the Suburbs", Broadcast: March 3rd, 2009 – 20:00

Ette, Andreas; Sauer, Lenore, "Abschied von Einwanderungsland Deutschland?-Die Migration Hochqualifizierter in europäischen und internationalen Vergleich", Bertlesmann Stiftung 2010, Gütersloh.

Florida, Richard: "Creative Class War", **Washington Monthly,** January 15, 2004, Online:www.alternet.org

Frangos, Alex: "What's New Urbanism Worth?", Wall Street Journal (Eastern edition), December 24, 2003, pg. B6.

Gardner, G.; Sampat, P., "Mind over Matter: Recasting the Role of Materials in our Lives", 1998

Gavin, Robert, "Getting a Lift—The Rockies Emerge as Pocket of Prosperity in a Slowing Economy", The Wall Street Journal, Wednesday, June 6, 2001.

Graham, Lamar, "Our Restored Cities, Where the Living is Easier", The Chicago Tribune—Parade Magazine, Sunday, April 25, 1999, pg. 4-5.

Graves, Clare W.: "Levels of Existence: An Open System Theory of Values", Journal of Humanistic Psychology, Fall 1970, Vol. 10 No. 2, pp. 131-155.

Graves, Clare W.: "Levels of Human Existence and their Relation to Value Analysis and Engineering", Transcript of the Fifth Annual Value Analysis Conference, 1964-1965, www.clarewgraves.com

Harden, Blaine: "Brain-Gain Cities Attract Educated Young", The Washington Post, November 9, 2003; Page A01

Inglehart, Ronald: "Culture and Democracy" in Harrison, Lawrence and Huntington, Samuel (eds.), Culture Matters: How Values Shape Human Progress, New York: Basic Books, 2000, pp. 80-97.

Inglehart, Ronald: "Globalization and Postmodern Values", The Washington Quarterly, 23(1), Winter 2000, pp. 215-228.

Jacobs, Karrie, http://www.metropolismag.com/ story/20050222/why-i-dont-love-richard-florida, Feb. 22, 2005

Kelling, George; Wilson, James Q.: "Broken Windows", Atlantic Monthly, March 1982, pp. 29-38.

Lee, William R.: "A Comparison of the Spiral Dynamics Map with other Maps", www.clarewgrave.com/research, September, 1999

Local Government Commission; United States Environmental Protection Agency, Creating Great Neighborhoods: Density in Your Community (pamphlet), National Association of Realtors, September 2003, pg. 7

Loftus, Peter, "Location, Location, Location", The Wall Street Journal, October 15, 2001, pg. R14

Niejahr, Elisabeth: „Die vergreiste Republik-Deutschland verliert jährlich 200000 Einwohner, da mehr Menschen sterben als geboren werden. Es wächst ein demografisches Problem ungeheuren Ausmaßes heran, doch die Politiker ignorieren es", DIE ZEIT, 02/2003.

Oberweis, Marcel: „Vernetztes Denken statt Fachwissen pur", Luxemburger Wort, January 17, 2004, Le marché national de l'emploi au Grand-Duché de Luxembourg, pg. 1.

Pfeffer, Jeffrey, „Danger: Toxic Company", Fast Company, November 19, 1998, pg 152
Roost, Frank: "Walt Disney's 'Celebration'. Die Amerikanische Stadt der Zukunft im Gewande der Vergangenheit", Die Alte Stadt, Heft 4/98, pp. 318-334.

Sachse, Katrin: „Null-Euro-Miese-Dorf; Eine Gemeinde schaffte das Wunder: Sie ist alle Schulden los und investiert Millionen", FOCUS 46/2003, pp. 54-57.

Schmidt-Bleek et al., "Statement to Government and Business Leaders", Wuppertal Institute, 1997.

United States Environmental Protection Agency, National Award for Smart Growth Achievement, 2003 (pamphlet), Office of Policy, Economics and Innovation (1808-T), EPA 231-F-03-002, November 2003
World Commission Urban 21, World Report on the Urban Future—Urban 21, pp.12-13.

Wientjes, Bernd: Alles in allem: Rosige Aussichten— TV Interview mit dem Zukunftsforscher Matthias Horx: Warum den Deutschen vor der Zukunft nicht bange sein muss, Trierischer Volksfreund, Nr. 303, Silvester 2003, Themen der Zeit: Wissenschaft, Seite 3

Verkehrs- und Verschönerungsverein, "Weimar, Guide to the City", Weimar, 1910.

Internet Addresses

http://www."Campaign for Sensible Growth"
  <listserv@growingsensibly.org

http://www.Curitiba,Brazil.htm

http://www.disneycelebrationfacts.com

http://www.earthcharter.org/wssd/

http://www.hometips.com

Holtzclaw, John, www.sierraclub.org/sprawl/
  articles/designing.asp

http://www.un.org/geninfo/bp/enviro.html

http://www.un.org/geninfo/bp/envirp2.html

http://www.un.org/geninfo/bp/envirp3.html

INDEX

Maslow, Abraham H. – 6, 13-14, 30, 34, 36, 42, 61, 102, 143-147, 149-151, 155-156, 161, 164, 167, 169-172, 179, 181-186, 188-189, 194, 196, 211

Materialistic – 171, 173, 175

Mediocrity – 34

Modern – 6, 25, 34, 36-37, 79-80, 209

Modernization – 36-42, 80, 209

National Center for Smart Growth Research and Education – 69

National Conference on Science, Policy and the Environment – 94

National Real Estate Board of the United States – 69

National Science Board – 48-49

Natural Capitalism – 5, 6, 61, 81-83, 86-89, 105, 114-115, 118-121, 125, 133-134, 199, 205, 209, 213

Neo-traditionalism – 70, 214-215

Neotraditionalists – 107

New Independent Problem Solvers – 11, 13-16, 20, 28-31, 34, 42-43, 46, 48, 50, 52-55, 57, 59, 60-61, 65, 71, 80, 86, 88, 102, 105, 111-113, 115, 122, 126, 131, 133, 179, 191, 195-198, 205

New Urbanism – 5, 12, 60-61, 67-71, 88-90, 107, 109, 111, 113-114, 122, 205, 208, 210, 215

New York – 78, 95-96, 98, 100-101, 123, 129-131, 183, 207, 214, 216

New York Transit Authority – 98

New Zealand – 103-104

Non-renewable resource – 123

Paradigm shift – 12, 82, 163

Physiological – 34, 149, 151-152, 155, 173

Plater-Zyberk, Elizabeth – 68, 111-112, 208

Post-materialists – 34, 40

Postmodern – 6, 40, 57, 68, 85, 124, 135, 184, 191, 216

Postmodernization – 36-42, 38, 41, 80, 209

Post-WWII – 22, 33, 38

Predatory man – 178

Proximity to nature – 44, 69, 112

Psychological development – 15, 53-54, 102, 153-154, 157-159, 160, 162, 171, 177, 180, 189, 198

225

226